Gold, Freedom, and Free Markets:

Economic Philosophy for Prudent Investors

Books for Business
New York - Hong Kong

Gold, Freedom, and Free Markets:
Economic Philosophy for Prudent Investors

by

Hans F. Sennholz
Murray N. Rothbard
Mark Skousen
et al.

ISBN: 0-89499-221-X

Books for Business
New York - Hong Kong
http://www.BusinessBooksInternational.com

Contents

Free Money - Is Sound Money

Hans F. Sennholz

RECENT ECONOMIC Developments reflect and portend the painful convulsions of our flat money system. The federal government is projecting a budget deficit of $34.7 billion for fiscal 1975 and a deficit of $51.9 billion for fiscal 1976. The U.S. Congress can be expected to boost federal spending even further which, together with the growing deficits of such "off-budget" agencies as the Postal Service and the Environmental Protection Agency, may raise the total federal deficit to more than $100 billion. State and local government deficits are making additional demands for economic resources. To finance such deficits out of the savings of the American people is well-nigh impossible. Therefore, the federal government may be expected to rely increasingly upon its monetary arm, the Federal Reserve System. Only hyper-inflation can finance super deficits.

A budgetary deficit is not just a temporary shortage of money that is readily covered by a loan. It is not primarily a monetary phenomenon that is efficiently handled by monetary authorities and bankers. Instead, a federal deficit means consumption of economic resources - real goods and services - beyond those taken directly from taxpayers. It consumes the real wealth and substance of savers who directly or indirectly buy the new Treasury obligations. The coming $100 billion deficit, in fact, greatly exceeds the annual savings of the American people, which were estimated to be $74.4 billion in 1973 and $76.7 billion in 1974. (Federal Reserve Bulletin, February, 1975, P. 57).

Redistributing Wealth

Whenever our savings are consumed by government, they obviously can no longer be used by individuals who would build or buy homes, household appliances, or make some other improvements. More facilities of production are used to serve government demand, fewer are left to cater to private demand. As the U.S. Treasury enters the capital market to sell its bills, notes and bonds, it absorbs and consumes the very substance of economic productivity. Its capital demand is felt as a chronic lack of capital for industry and commerce, for public utilities, for development of more energy, modernization and renovation and new production facilities. It is felt as a universal "shortage of funds" which, in reality, is a shortage of real savings and economic resources. Plagued by such shortages and enmeshed in serious economic difficulties and crises, the federal government then calls on the Federal Reserve System to alleviate the shortages through credit expansion and money creation. Tons of new paper money are thus to take the place of real goods that are consumed by our political organizations.

The inevitable rise in prices of goods, commonly called inflation, then serves to withdraw the resources from certain individuals and redirects them to the spender with the newly created purchasing power, the federal government. Inflation acts as a federal tax on all holders of money and claims to money. It silently and efficiently transfers real income and wealth from millions of individuals to the inflating government. Nor do most of the victims understand the nature of this taxing process. After all, rising prices can be blamed on merchants and industrialists, thus exculpating the government that is withdrawing and consuming the economic resources. The very administration that is conducting such policies may even blame businessmen for the inflation and proceed to impose price and wage controls on its victims.

A Tool of Politics

In the coming years of galloping inflation the American people may come to understand the true nature of the fiat system that makes government the creator and guardian of money. They may learn what the defenders of gold as money knew all along, that fiat money is political money - an effective tool for the financial aspirations of political parties and administrations. Fiat money serves as an important implement, not only for such policies as "full employment" and "economic growth," but also for massive redistribution of economic wealth from creditors to debtors. Fiat money is the political device ideally suited to achieve the transfer of income and wealth on a gigantic scale.

Inflation that gradually erodes the capital substance of the middle class can be effective in the fog of political confusion and economic ignorance. In a few years of double-digit inflation, the savings bonds, pension funds, life insurance policies and even corporate stock holdings which constitute the very substance of the middle class, are consumed by government or transferred into the possession of debtors. Massive deficits financed by double-digit inflation thus sustain the redistributive society that heretofore depended mainly on confiscatory taxation of its richer members,

The proceeds of inflation as a tax on monetary assets accrue not only to the government that is actively inflating the currency but also to all other debtors, including corporations and individuals. When the dollar depreciates, all creditors lose while all debtors gain, whether they are political organizations or corporations. Economic property is redistributed universally from a large class of victims, commonly the middle class, to the political institutions and a new class of nouveaux riches, which is enjoying the fall-out effects of inflation. We need not emphasize here that such policies create new sources of economic conflict and social strife.

Yearning for Stability

The yearning of the people of America for "stable money" is a natural reaction to the painful experience of unprecedented instability. The task of philosophers, jurists, historians, and economists is to explain the alternative to the fiat system, to teach the virtues and advantages of natural money which is also honest money. If people who work and trade are free to choose between political fiat and gold or silver, they naturally turn to the precious metals. They choose the gold standard as a monetary system in which gold is proper money and all paper moneys are merely substitutes that are payable in gold. This makes the U.S. dollar a piece of gold of a certain weight and fineness.

But it is a popular mistake that is shared by many historians and economists alike that the gold standard affords monetary stability and that gold coins are endowed with unchanging purchasing power. In a changing world of human action, no money can be neutral or stable. Even a 100 per cent hard-money gold standard, in which the currency of each country would consist exclusively of gold, cannot afford stability of purchasing power to its gold coins. Just as the price of an economic good is ultimately determined by the subjective valuation of buyers and sellers, so is the purchasing power of money. Individual valuation of money is subject to the same considerations of demand and supply as that of all other goods and services. People expend labor or forgo the enjoyment of other economic goods in order to acquire money. At times they bid for money, at other times they offer money, and all this bidding and offering ultimately determines the purchasing power of money in the same way as it determines the mutual exchange ratios of other goods.

All plans to make money stable are contradictory to human nature and dangerous to individual freedom, as they would call on government to enforce the impossible. The yearning for "stable money," therefore, is forever futile unless it means to want honest money that is free from the political processes of public treasuries and central banks. The best we can hope for is monetary freedom that embodies the freedom of contract and choice of money. In freedom, the American people once again could express their preference for gold and silver coins over depreciating political fiat.

A Crucial Choice

Our choice of a monetary system is of crucial importance. Do we want a system in which government creates and manages money through the political process? Or do we prefer to leave that choice to acting people who are exchanging goods and services on the market? If we rely on government we must be prepared to live with government fiat, which is ideally suited to serve political ends. Fiat money can be expanded or contracted at will, always accommodating the national policy of the moment. Above all, it can be inflated at will to supplement government revenue.

On the other hand, if buyers and sellers are free to make the selection they may choose a great variety of marketable goods as their media of exchange. In the past, in a selective process extending over several thousand years, they chose the precious metals, gold and silver, as their money. Are they no longer to be trusted with such freedom of choice?

Government need not establish the gold standard by any conscious or deliberate act. In fact, the gold standard needs neither rules nor regulations, no legislation or government control, merely the individual freedom to own gold. Of course, this freedom of gold ownership embodies the freedom not only to buy and sell gold for use in industrial production, but also to employ it in exchange.

The gold-coin standard means sound money. It is true, it cannot achieve the unattainable ideal of an absolutely stable currency. But it protects the monetary system from the influence of governments. The quantity of gold in existence is utterly independent of the wishes and manipulations of government officials and politicians, parties and pressure groups. There are no arbitrary "rules of the game," which people must learn to observe. The gold standard is a social institution that is controlled by inexorable economic law.

Fully Redeemable

The issuers of money substitutes keep their currencies at par with gold through unconditional redemption. The issuing bank can buy any amount of gold offered to it at the parity rate, and agrees to sell indiscriminately and on demand any amount of gold against its notes or deposits. It thereby renders no national service in the sense of "defending" or "Protecting" its currency. It merely fulfills the contract it made when it issued the money substitutes.

Under the gold-coin standard, inflationary policies are not rendered impossible, but they are made difficult. Redemption requirements and the threat of drains of their gold reserves would restrain the issuers of money substitutes from inflationary expansion. For any such expansion would alarm the owners of substitutes and cause them to demand redemption in gold coin, which would spell ruin to the issuer. As the gold standard makes inflationary policies difficult, it avoids the wide fluctuations of economic activity, known as the business cycle. This binds the issuers of money substitutes within very narrow limits, and thus efficiently checks the sort of credit expansion that creates great instability and generates the economic boom and bust cycle.[1]

Professor William Graham Sumner, the great Yale economist of the pre-Federal Reserve era, described the instability of irredeemable paper currency as follows: "Scheme after scheme has been proposed and tried for realizing the gain which it was believed that cheap money could produce for the public; that is, for those who buy and use currency. This gain has been pursued as the alchemists pursued the philosopher's stone, by trial and failure. Whether there be any such gain or not, our attempts to win it have all failed, and they have cost us, in each generation, more than a purely specie currency would have cost, if each generation had had to buy it anew. . . . The revulsion-, to which the system was subject overwhelmed us in every decade. The notions on which the system was based are proved to have been delusion, disastrous to everybody concerned, including those who tried to profit by them,"[2]

A World Market

The international gold standard evolved without intergovernmental treaties and institutions. No one had to make the gold standard work as an international system. When the leading nations of the world had adopted gold as their currency, the world had an international money. It is true, the coins bore different names and had different weights. But this hardly mattered as long as they consisted of gold and could be exchanged freely. After all, an ounce of gold is an ounce of gold whether it consists of eagles or sovereigns.

The gold standard united the world as it overcame the problem of international payments. It facilitated international trade and finance, and thereby promoted a world-wide division of labor. Countries specialized in producing those internationally traded commodities which afforded them the greatest comparative advantage. But above all, the gold standard encouraged exportation of capital from the industrial countries to the backward areas. Without fear of devaluation losses or transfer restrictions, European capital eagerly sought profitable employment opportunities on all continents. It developed commerce and industry and thus improved working and living conditions all over the globe.

The history of the gold standard heralds the principles and achievements of free and honest money, The history of fiat money is little more than a register of monetary follies and inflations. Current affairs afford but another entry in this dismal register. We may hope for an early return of monetary freedom and sound money, but realization is hidden in the dark clouds of the future, Sound money is the most prominent concomitant of economic freedom and morality; fiat money is an inevitable symptom of their absence.

The duty of each of us is to understand and explain as best he can the principles of economic freedom and honest money. Our future depends on it.

About the Author

At the time of the original publication, Dr. Sennholz headed the Department of Economics at Grove City College and is a noted writer and lecturer on monetary and economic affairs.

This article is published by permission from a paper before a meeting of the Committee for Monetary Research and Education, March 22, 1975.

[1] *Ludwig von Mises, Human Action, Yale University Press, 1949, p. 535 et seq.*

[2] *William Craham Sumner, History of Banking in the U.S., New York: The Journal of Commerce and Commercial Bulletin, 1896, p. 472.*

Reprinted with permission from The Freeman, a publication of The Foundation for Economic Education, Inc., June, 1975, Vol. 25, No. 6.

The Solution

Murray N. Rothbard

To save our economy from destruction and from the eventual holocaust of runaway inflation, we the people must take the money-supply function back from the government. Money is far too important to be left in the hands of bankers and of Establishment economists and financiers. To accomplish this goal, money must be returned to the market economy, with all monetary functions performed within the structure of the rights of private property and of the free-market economy.

It might be thought that the mix of government and money is too far gone, too pervasive in the economic system, too inextricably bound up in the economy, to be eliminated without economic destruction. Conservatives are accustomed to denouncing the "terrible simplifiers" who wreck everything by imposing simplistic and unworkable schemes, Our major problem, however, is precisely the opposite: mystification by the ruling elite of technocrats and intellectuals, who, whenever some public spokesman arises to call for large-scale tax cuts or deregulation, intone sarcastically about the dimwit masses who "seek simple solutions for complex problems." Well, in most cases, the solutions are indeed clear-cut and simple, but are deliberately obfuscated by people whom we might call "terrible complicators." In truth, taking back our money would be relatively simple and straightforward, much less difficult than the daunting task of denationalizing and de-communizing the Communist countries of Eastern Europe and the former Soviet Union.

Our goal may be summed up simply as the privatization of our monetary system, the separation of government from money and banking. The central means to accomplish this task is also straightforward: the abolition, the liquidation of the Federal Reserve System - the abolition of central banking. How could the Federal Reserve System possibly be abolished? Elementary: simply repeal its federal charter, the Federal Reserve Act of 1913. Moreover, Federal Reserve obligations (its notes and deposits) were originally redeemable in gold on demand. Since Franklin Roosevelt's monstrous actions in 1933, "dollars" issued by the Federal Reserve, and deposits by the Fed and its member banks, have no longer been redeemable in gold. Bank deposits are redeemable in Federal Reserve Notes, while Federal Reserve Notes are redeemable in nothing, or alternatively in other Federal Reserve Notes. Yet, these Notes are our money, our monetary "standard," and all creditors are obliged to accept payment in these fiat notes, no matter how depreciated they might be.

In addition to cancelling the redemption of dollars into gold, Roosevelt in 1933 committed another criminal act: literally confiscating all gold and bullion held by Americans, exchanging them for arbitrarily valued "dollars." It is curious that, even though the Fed and the government establishment continually proclaim the obsolescence and worthlessness of gold as a monetary metal, the Fed (as well as all other central banks) clings to its gold for dear life. Our confiscated gold is still owned by the Federal Reserve, which keeps it on deposit with the Treasury at Fort Knox and other gold depositaries. Indeed, from 1933 until the 1970s, it continued to be illegal for any Americans to own monetary gold of any kind, whether coin or bullion or even in safe deposit boxes at home or abroad. All these measures, supposedly drafted for the Depression emergency, have continued as part of the great heritage of the New Deal ever since. For four decades, any gold flowing into private American hands had to be deposited in the banks, which in turn had to deposit it at the Fed. Gold for "legitimate" non-monetary purposes, such as dental fillings, industrial drills, or jewelry, was carefully rationed for such purposes by the Treasury Department.

Fortunately, due to the heroic efforts of Congressman Ron Paul it is now legal for Americans to own gold, whether coin or bullion. But the ill-gotten gold confiscated and sequestered by the Fed remains in Federal Reserve hands. How to get the gold out from the Fed? How privatize the Fed's stock of gold?

Privatizing Federal Gold

The answer is revealed by the fact that the Fed, which had promised to redeem its liabilities in gold, has been in default of that promise since Roosevelt's repudiation of the gold standard in 1933. The Federal Reserve System, being in default, should be liquidated, and the way to liquidate it is the way any insolvent business firm is liquidated: its assets are parceled out, pro rata, to its creditors. The Federal Reserve's gold assets are listed, as of October 30, 1991, at $11.1 billion. The Federal Reserve's liabilities as of that date consist of $295.5 billion in Federal Reserve Notes in circulation, and $24.4 billion in deposits owed to member banks of the Federal Reserve System, for a total of $319.9 billion. Of the assets of the Fed, other than gold, the bulk are securities of the U.S. government, which amounted to $262.5 billion. These should be written off posthaste, since they are worse than an accounting fiction: the taxpayers are forced to pay interest and principle on debt which the Federal Government owes to its own creature, the Federal Reserve. The largest remaining asset is Treasury Currency, $21.0 billion, which should also be written off, plus $10 billion in SDRs, which are mere paper creatures of international central banks, and which should be abolished as well. We are left (apart from various buildings and fixtures and other assets owned by the Fed, and amounting to some $35 billion) with $11.1 billion of assets needed to pay off liabilities totalling $319.9 billion.

Fortunately, the situation is not as dire as it seems, for the $11.1 billion of Fed gold is a purely phoney evaluation; indeed it is one of the most bizarre aspects of our fraudulent monetary system. The Fed's gold stock consists of 262.9 million ounces of gold; the dollar valuation of $11.1 billion is the result of the government's artificially evaluating its own stock of gold at $42.22 an ounce. Since the market price of gold is now about $350 an ounce, this already presents a glaring anomaly in the system.

Definitions and Debasement

Where did the $42.22 come from?

The essence of a gold standard is that the monetary unit (the "dollar," "franc," "mark," etc.) is defined as a certain weight of gold. Under the gold standard, the dollar or franc is not a thing-in-itself, a mere name or the name of a paper ticket issued by the State or a central bank; it is the name of a unit of weight of gold. It is every bit as much a unit of weight as the more general - ounce," "grain," or "gram." For a century before 1933, the "dollar" was defined as being equal to 23.22 grains of gold; since there are 480 grains to the ounce, this meant that the dollar was also defined as .048 gold ounce. Put another way, the gold ounce was defined as equal to $20.67.

In addition to taking us off the gold standard domestically, Franklin Roosevelt's New Deal "debased" the dollar by redefining it, or "lightening its weight," as equal to 13.714 grains of gold, which also defined the gold ounce as equal to $35. The dollar was still redeemable in gold to foreign central banks and governments at the lighter $35 weight; so that the United States stayed on a hybrid form of international gold standard until August 1971, when President Nixon completed the job of scuttling the gold standard altogether. Since 1971, the United States has been on a totally flat paper standard; not coincidentally, it has suffered an unprecedented degree of peace-time inflation since that date. Since 197 1, the dollar has no longer been tied to gold at a fixed weight, and so it has become a commodity separate from gold, free to fluctuate on world markets.

When the dollar and gold were set loose from each other, we saw the closest thing to a laboratory experiment we can get in human affairs. All Establishment economists-from Keynesians to Chicagoite monetarists-insisted that gold had long lost its value as a money, that gold had only reached its exalted value of $35 an ounce because its value was "fixed" at that amount by the government. The dollar allegedly conferred value upon gold rather than the other way round, and if gold and the dollar were ever cut loose, we would see the price of gold sink rapidly to its estimated non-monetary value (for jewelry, dental fillings, etc.) of approximately $6 an ounce. In contrast to this unanimous Establishment prediction, the followers of Ludwig von Mises and other "gold bugs" insisted that gold was undervalued at 35 debased dollars, and claimed that the price of gold would rise far higher, perhaps as high as $70.

Suffice it to say that the gold price never fell below $35, and in fact vaulted upward, at one point reaching $850 an ounce, in recent years settling at somewhere around $350 an ounce. And yet since 1973, the Treasury and Fed have persistently evaluated their gold stock, not at the old and obsolete $35, to be sure, but only slightly higher, at $42.22 an ounce. In other words, if the U.S. government only made the simple adjustment that accounting requires of everyone- evaluating one's assets at their market price-the value of the Fed's gold stock would immediately rise from $11.1 to $92.0 billion.

From 1933 to 1971, the once very large but later dwindling number of economists championing a return to the gold standard mainly urged a return to $35 an ounce. Mises and his followers advocated a higher gold "price," inasmuch as the $35 rate no longer applied to Americans. But the majority did have a point: that any measure or definition, once adopted, should be adhered to from then on. But since 1971, with the death of the once-sacred $35 an ounce, all bets are off. While definitions once adopted should be maintained permanently, there is nothing sacred about any initial definition, which should be selected at its most useful point. If we wish to restore the gold standard, we are free to select whatever definition of the dollar is most useful; there are no longer any obligations to the obsolete definitions of $20.67 or $35 an ounce.

Abolishing the Fed

In particular, if we wish to liquidate the Federal Reserve System, we can select a new definition of the "dollar" sufficient to pay off all Federal Reserve liabilities at 100 cents to the dollar. In the case of our example above, we can now redefine "the dollar" as equivalent to 0.394 grains of gold, or as 1 ounce of gold equalling $1,217. With such redefinition, the entire Federal Reserve stock of gold could be minted by the Treasury into gold coins that would replace the Federal Reserve Notes in circulation, and also constitute gold coin reserves of $24.4 billion at the various commercial banks. The Federal Reserve System would be abolished, gold coins would now be in circulation replacing Federal Reserve Notes, gold would be the circulating medium, and gold dollars the unit of account and reckoning, at the new rate of $1,217 per ounce. Two great desiderata-the return of the gold standard, and the abolition of the Federal Reserve-would both be accomplished at one stroke.

A corollary step, of course, would be the abolition of the already bankrupt Federal Deposit Insurance Corporation. The very concept of "deposit insurance" is fraudulent; how can you "insure" an entire industry that is inherently insolvent? It would be like insuring the Titanic after it hit the iceberg. Some free-market economists advocate "privatizing" deposit insurance by encouraging private firms, or the banks themselves, to "insure" each others' deposits. But that would return us to the unsavory days of Florentine bank cartels, in which every bank tried to shore up each other's liabilities. It won't work; let us not forget that the first S & Ls to collapse in the 1980s were those in Ohio and in Maryland, which enjoyed the dubious benefits of "private" deposit insurance.

This issue points up an important error often made by libertarians and free-market economists who believe that all government activities should be privatized; or as a corollary, hold that any actions, so long as they are private, are legitimate. But, on the contrary, activities such as fraud, embezzlement, or counterfeiting should not be "privatized"; they should be abolished.

This would leave the commercial banks still in a state of fractional reserve, and, in the past, I have advocated going straight to 100 percent, non-fraudulent banking by raising the gold price enough to constitute 100 percent of bank demand liabilities. After that, of course, 100 percent banking would be legally required. At current estimates, establishing 100 percent to all commercial bank demand deposit accounts would require going back to gold at $2,000 an ounce; to include all checkable deposits would require establishing gold at $3,350 an ounce, and to establish 100 percent banking for all checking and savings deposits (which are treated by everyone as redeemable on demand) would require a gold standard at $7,500 an ounce.

But there are problems with such a solution. A minor problem is that the higher the newly established gold value over the current market price, the greater the consequent increase in gold production. This increase would cause an admittedly modest and one-shot price inflation. A more important problem is the moral one: do banks deserve what amounts to a free gift, in which the Fed, before liquidating, would bring every bank's gold assets high enough to be 100 percent of its liabilities? Clearly, the banks scarcely deserve such benign treatment, even in the name of smoothing the transition to sound money; bankers should consider themselves lucky they are not tried for embezzlement. Furthermore, it would be difficult to enforce and police 100 percent banking on an administrative basis. It would be easier, and more libertarian, to go through the courts. Before the Civil War, the notes of unsound fractional reserve banks in the United States, if geographically far from home base, were bought up at a discount by professional "money brokers," who would then travel to the banks' home base and demand massive redemption of these notes in gold.

The same could be done today, and more efficiently, using advanced electronic technology, as professional money brokers try to make profits by detecting unsound banks and bringing them to heel. A particular favorite of mine is the concept of ideological Anti-Bank Vigilante Leagues, who would keep tabs on banks, spot the errant ones, and go on television to proclaim that banks are unsound, and urge note and deposit holders to call upon them for redemption without delay. If the Vigilante Leagues could whip up hysteria and consequent bank runs, in which note-holders and depositors scramble to get their money out before the bank goes under, then so much the better: for then, the people themselves, and not simply the government, would ride herd on fractional reserve banks. The important point, it must be emphasized, is that at the very first sign of a bank's failing to redeem its notes or deposits on demand, the police and courts must put them out of business. Instant justice, period, with no mercy and no bailouts.

Under such a regime, it should not take long for the banks to go under, or else to contract their notes and deposits until they are down to 100 percent banking. Such monetary deflation, while leading to various adjustments, would be clearly one-shot, and would obviously have to stop permanently when the total of bank liabilities contracted down to 100 percent of gold assets. One crucial difference between inflation and deflation, is that inflation can escalate up to an infinity of money supply and prices, whereas the money supply can only deflate as far as the total amount of standard money, under the gold standard the supply of gold money. Gold constitutes an absolute floor against further deflation.

If this proposal seems harsh on the banks, we have to realize that the banking system is headed for a mighty crash in any case. As a result of the S&L collapse, the terribly shaky nature of our banking system is at last being realized. People are openly talking of the FDIC being insolvent, and of the entire banking structure crashing to the ground. And if the people ever get to realize this in their bones, they will precipitate a mighty "bank run" by trying to get their money out of the banks and into their own pockets. And the banks would then come tumbling down, because the people's money isn't there. The only thing that could save the banks in such a mighty bank run is if the Federal Reserve prints the $1.6 trillion in cash and gives it to the banks-igniting an immediate and devastating runaway inflation and destruction of the dollar.

Liberals are fond of blaming our economic crisis on the "greed of the 1980s." And yet "greed" was no more intense in the 1980s than it was in the 1970s or previous decades or than it will be in the future. What happened in the 1980s was a virulent episode of government deficits and of Federal Reserve-inspired credit expansion by the banks. As the Fed purchased assets and pumped in reserves to the banking system, the banks happily multiplied bank credit and created new money on top of those reserves.

There has been a lot of focus on poor quality bank loans: on loans to bankrupt Third World countries or to bloated and, in retrospect, unsound real estate schemes and shopping malls in the middle of nowhere. But poor quality loans and investments are always the consequence of central bank and bank-credit expansion. The all—too-familiar cycle of boom and bust, euphoria and crash, prosperity and depression, did not begin in the 1980s. Nor is it a creature of civilization or the market economy. The boom-bust cycle began in the eighteenth century with the beginnings of central banking, and has spread and intensified ever since, as central banking spread and took control of the economic systems of the Western world. Only the abolition of the Federal Reserve System and a return to the gold standard can put an end to cyclical booms and busts, and finally eliminate chronic and accelerating inflation.

Inflation, credit expansion, business cycles, heavy government debt, and high taxes are not, as Establishment historians claim, inevitable attributes of capitalism or of -modernization.- On the contrary, these are profoundly anti-capitalist and parasitic excrescences grafted onto the system by the interventionist State, which rewards its banker and insider clients with hidden special privileges at the expense of everyone else.

Crucial to free enterprise and capitalism is a system of firm rights of private property, with everyone secure in the property that he earns. Also crucial to capitalism is an ethic that encourages and rewards savings, thrift, hard work, and productive enterprise, and that discourages profligacy and cracks down sternly on any invasion of property rights. And yet, as we have seen, cheap money and credit expansion gnaw away at those rights and at those virtues. Inflation overturns and trans-values values by rewarding the spendthrift and the inside fixer and by making a mockery of the older "Victorian" virtues.

Restoring the Old Republic

The restoration of American liberty and of the Old Republic is a multi-faceted task. It requires excising the cancer of the Leviathan State from our midst. It requires removing Washington, D.C., as the power center of the country. It requires restoring the ethics and virtues of the nineteenth century, the taking back of our culture from nihilism and victimology, and restoring that culture to health and sanity. In the long run, politics, culture, and the economy are indivisible. The restoration of the Old Republic requires an economic system built solidly on the inviolable rights of private property, on the right of every person to keep what he earns, and to exchange the products of his labor. To accomplish that task, we must once again have money that is produced on the market, that is gold rather than paper, with the monetary unit a weight of gold rather than the name of a paper ticket issued ad lib by the government. We must have investment determined by voluntary savings on the market, and not by counterfeit money and credit issued by a knavish and State—privileged banking system. In short, we must abolish central banking, and force the banks to meet their obligations as promptly as anyone else. Money and banking have been made to appear as mysterious and arcane processes that must be guided and operated by a technocratic elite. They are nothing of the sort. In money, even more than the rest of our affairs, we have been tricked by a malignant Wizard of Oz. In money, as in other areas of our lives, restoring common sense and the Old Republic go hand in hand.

About the Author

Murray N. Rothbard (1926-1995) was the S. J. Hall Distinguished Professor of Economics at the University of Nevada, Las Vegas, and Academic Vice President of the Ludwig von Mises Institute.

Reprinted with permission from The Freeman, a publication of the Foundation for Economic Education, Inc., November 1995, Vol. 45, No. 11.

A Golden Comeback

Mark Skousen

"A more timeless measure is
needed; gold fits the bill
perfectly."

--Mark Mobius

When speaking of the Midas metal, I'm reminded of Mark Twain's refrain, "The reports of my death are greatly exaggerated." After years of central-bank selling and a bear market in precious metals, the Financial Times recently declared the "Death of Gold." But is it dead?

Following the Asian financial crisis last year, Mark Mobius, the famed Templeton manager of emerging markets, advocated the creation of a new regional currency, the asian, convertible to gold, including the issuance of Asian gold coins. "All their M1 money supply and foreign reserves would be converted into asians at the current price of gold. Henceforth asians would be issued only upon deposits of gold or foreign-currency equivalents of gold." [1] Mobius castigated the central banks of Southeast Asia for recklessly depreciating their currencies. As a result, "many businesses and banks throughout the region have become bankrupt, billions of dollars have been lost, and economic development has been threatened." Why gold? "Because gold has always been a store of value in Asia and is respected as the last resort in times of crisis. Asia's history is strewn with fallen currencies. ... The beauty of gold is that it limits a country's ability to spend to the amount it can earn in addition to its gold holdings."

Not Just Another Commodity

Recent studies give support to Mobius's new monetary proposal. According to these studies, gold has three unique features: First, gold provides a stable numeraire for the world's monetary system, one that closely matches the "monetarist rule." Second, gold has had an amazing capacity to maintain its purchasing power throughout history, what the late Roy Jastram called "The Golden Constant." And, third, the yellow metal has a curious ability to predict future inflation and interest rates.

Let's start with gold as a stable monetary system. With most commodities, such as wheat or oil, the "carryover" stocks vary significantly with annual production. Not so with gold. Historical data confirm that the aggregate gold stockpile held by individuals and central banks always increases and never declines. [2] Moreover, the annual increase in the world gold stock typically varies between 1.5 and 3 percent, and seldom exceeds 3 percent. In short, the gradual increase in the stock of gold closely resembles the "monetary rule" cherished by Milton Friedman and the monetarists, where the money stock rises at a steady rate (see Chart I).

Compare the stability of the gold supply with the annual changes in the paper money supply held by central banks. As Chart II indicates, the G-7 money-supply index rose as much as 17 percent in the early 1970s and as little as 3 percent in the 1990s. (Why has monetary growth slowed, even under a fiat money standard? The financial markets, especially the bondholders, have demanded fiscal restraint of their governments.) Moreover, the central banks' monetary policies were far more volatile than the gold supply. On a worldwide basis, gold proved to be more stable and less inflationary than a fiat money system.

Critics agree that gold is inherently a "hard" currency, but complain that new gold production can't keep up with economic growth. In other words, gold is too much of a hard currency. As noted, the world gold stock rises at a miserly annual growth rate of less than 3 percent and often times under 2 percent, while GDP growth usually exceeds 3 or 4 percent and sometimes 7 or 8 percent in developing nations. The result? Price deflation is inevitable under a pure gold standard. My response: Critics are right that gold-supply growth is not likely to keep up with real GDP growth. Only during major gold discoveries, such as in California and Australia in the 1850s or South Africa in the 1890s, did world gold supplies grow faster than 4 percent a year. [3]

Prices Must Be Flexible

Consequently, an economy working under a pure gold standard will suffer gradual deflation; the price level will probably decline 1 to 3 percent a year, depending on gold production and economic growth. But price deflation isn't such a bad thing as long as it is gradual and not excessive. There have been periods of strong economic growth accompanying a general price deflation, such as the 1890s, 1920s, and 1950s. But price and wage flexibility is essential to make it work.

About The Author

At the time of the original publication, Dr. Skousen was an economist at Rollins College, Department of Economics, Winter Park, Florida 32789, a Forbes columnist, and editor of Forecasts & Strategies. He is also the author of Economics on Trial (Irwin, 1993), a review of the top ten textbooks in economics.

[1]. *Mark Mobius, "Asia Needs a Single Currency," Wall Street Journal, February 19, 1998, p. A22.*

[2]. *See the chart on page 84 of my Economics of a Pure Gold Standard, 3rd ed. (1997), available from FEE. Note how the world monetary stock of gold never has declined between 1810 and 1933.*

[3]. *Ibid., p. 96.*

Reprinted with permission from The Freeman, a publication of the Foundation for Economic Education, Inc., September 1998, Vol. 48, No. 9.

A Golden Comeback, Part II

Mark Skousen

> "Gold maintains its purchasing power over long periods of time, for example, half-century intervals."
>
> --*Roy Jastram, The Golden Constant* [1]

In last month's column, I focused on gold's inherent stability as a monetary numeraire. Historically, the monetary base under gold has neither declined nor increased too rapidly. In short, it has operated very closely to a monetarist rule.

What about gold as an inflation hedge? In this column, I discuss the work of Roy Jastram and others who have demonstrated the relative stability of gold in terms of its purchasing power-its ability to maintain value and purchasing power over goods and services over the long run. But the emphasis must be placed on the "long run." In the short run, gold's value depends a great deal on the rate of inflation and therefore often fails to live up to its reputation as an inflation hedge.

The classic study on the purchasing power of gold is The Golden Constant: The English and American Experience, 1560-1976, by Roy W Jastram, late professor of business at the University of

California, Berkeley, The book, now out of print, examines gold as an inflation and deflation hedge over a span of 400 years.

Two Amazing Graphs

The accompanying two charts are from Jastram's book and updated through 1997 by the American Institute for Economic Research in Great Barrington, Massachusetts. They tell a powerful story:

First, gold always returns to its full purchasing power, although it may take a long time to do so; and Second, the price of gold became more volatile as the world moved to a fiat money standard beginning in the 1930s. Note how gold has moved up and down sharply as the pound and the dollar have lost purchasing power since going off the gold standard.

In my economics classes and at investment conferences, I demonstrate the long-term value of gold by holding up a $20 St. Gaudens double-eagle gold coin. Prior to 1933, Americans carried this coin in their pockets as money. Back then, they could buy a tailor-made suit for one double eagle, or $20. Today this same coin - which is worth between $400 and $600, depending on its rarity and condition - could buy the same tailor-made suit. Of course, the double-eagle coin has numismatic, or rarity, value. A one-ounce gold-bullion coin, without numismatic value, is worth only around $300 today. Gold has risen substantially in dollar terms but has not done as well as numismatic U.S. coins.

Gold as an Inflation Hedge

The price of gold bullion was over $800 an ounce in 1980 and has steadily declined in value for nearly two decades. Does that mean it's not a good inflation hedge? Indeed, the record shows that when the inflation rate is steady or declining, gold has been a poor hedge. The yellow metal (and mining shares) typically responds best to accelerating inflation. Over the long run, the Midas metal has held its own, but should not be deemed an ideal or perfect hedge. In fact, U.S. stocks have proven to be much profitable than gold as an investment.

The work of Jeremy Siegel, professor of finance at the Wharton School of the University of Pennsylvania, has demonstrated that U.S. stocks have far outperformed gold over the past two centuries. Like Jastram, Siegel confirms gold's long-term stability. Yet gold can't hold a candle to the stock market's performance. As the chart, taken from his book, Stocks for the Long Term, shows, stocks have far outperformed bonds, T-bills, and gold. Why? Because stocks represent higher economic growth and productivity over the long run. Stocks have risen sharply in the twentieth century because of a dramatic rise in the standard of living and America's free-enterprise system.

One final note: Stocks tend to do poorly and gold shines when price inflation accelerates. As Siegel states, "Stocks turn out to be great long-term hedges against inflation even though they are often poor short-term hedges." [2] Price inflation is the key indicator: then the rate of inflation moves back up, watch out. Stocks could flounder and gold will come back to life. In my next column, I'll discuss the ability of gold to predict inflation and interest rates.

About the Author

At the time of the original publication, Dr. Skousen was an economist at Rollins College, Department of Economics, Winter Park, Florida 32789, a Forbes columnist, and editor of Forecasts & Strategies, He is also the author of Economics of a Pure Gold Standard, 3rd edition (Foundation for Economic Education, 1996, and was working on his own textbook, Economic Logic.

[1] *Roy W. Jastram, The Golden Constant: The English and American Experience, 1560-1976 (New York: Wiley & Sons, 1977), p. 132.*

[2] *Jeremy J. Siegel, Stocks for the Long Run: A Guide to Selecting Markets for Long-Term Growth (Burr Ridge, Ill.: Irwin, 1994), pp. 11-12.*

Reprinted with permission from The Freeman, a publication of The Foundation for Economic Education, Inc., October 1998, Vol. 48, No. 10.

A Golden Comeback, Part III

Mark Skousen

> "A free gold market ... reflects
> and measures the extent of the
> lack of confidence in the
> domestic currency."

--Ludwig von Mises

In the past two columns, I've highlighted the uses and misuses of gold. Despite occasional calls for a return to a gold standard, the Midas metal has largely lost out to hard currencies as a preferred monetary unit and monetary reserve. Most central banks are selling gold.

Gold has also done poorly as a crisis hedge lately. It has not rallied much during recent wars and international incidents. U.S. Treasury securities and hard currencies such as the German mark and Swiss franc have become the investments of choice in a flight to safety Nor has gold functioned well as an inflation hedge over the past two decades. The cost of living continues to increase around the world, yet the price of gold has fallen from $800 an ounce in 1980 to under $300 today.

What's left for the yellow metal? I see two essential functions for gold: first, a profitable investment when general prices accelerate and, second, an important barometer of future price inflation and interest rates.

Gold as a Profitable Investment

Since the United States went off the gold standard in 1971, gold bullion and gold mining shares have become well-known cyclical investments. The first graph demonstrates the volatile nature of gold and mining stocks, with mining shares tending to fluctuate more than gold itself. The gold industry can provide superior profits during an uptrend, and heavy losses during a downtrend.

One of the reasons for the high volatility of mining shares is their distance from final consumption. Mining represents the earliest stage of production and is extremely capital intensive and responsive to changes in interest rates. [1]

Gold as a Forecaster

Gold also has the amazingly accurate ability to forecast the direction of the general price level and interest rates. In an earlier Freeman column (February 1997), I referred to an econometric model I ran with the assistance of John List, economist at the University of Central Florida. We tested three commodity indexes (Dow Jones Commodity Spot Index, crude oil, and gold) to determine which one best anticipated changes in the Consumer Price Index (CPI) since 1970. It turned out that gold proved to be the best indicator of future inflation as measured by the CPI. The tag period is about one year. That is, gold does a good job of predicting the direction of the CPI a year in advance. (All three indexes did a poor job of predicting changes in the CPI on a monthly basis.)

Richard M. Salsman, economist at H. C. Wainwright & Co. in Boston, has also done some important work linking the price of gold with interest rates. As the second graph demonstrates, the price of gold often anticipates changes in interest rates in the United States. As Salsman states, "A rising gold price presages higher bond yields; a falling price signals lower yields.... Gold predicts yields well precisely because it's a top-down measure. It is bought and sold based purely on inflation-deflation expectations; thus it's the purest barometer of changes in the value of the dollar generally." [2]

In sum, if you want to know the future of inflation and interest rates, watch the gold traders at the New York Merc. If gold enters a sustained rise, watch out: higher inflation and interest rates may be on the way.

About the Author

At the time of the original publication, Dr. Skousen was an economist at Rollins College, Department of Economics, Winter Park, Florida 32789, a Forbes columnist, and editor of Forecasts & Strategies. He is also the author of "Economics of a Pure Gold Standard", 3rd Edition (Foundation for Economic Education, 1996), and He was working on his own textbook "Economic Logic".

[1] *For further discussion regarding the inherent volatility of the mining industry, see my work The Structure of Production (New York: New York University Press, 1990), pp. 290-94.*

[2] *Richard M. Salsman, "Looking for Inflation in All the Wrong Places," The Capitalist Perspective (Boston: H. C. Wainwright & Co. Economics), October 15, 1997. For information on his services, call (800) 655-4020.*

Reprinted with permission from The Freeman, a publication of The Foundation for Economic Education, Inc., November 1998, Vol. 48, No. 11.

The Great Gold Robbery

James Bovard

Some of the programs and policies of that era have been terminated, the moral heritage of the New Deal continues to permeate American government and political thinking.

In 1936 Franklin Roosevelt declared, "I should like to have it said of my first Administration that in it the forces of selfishness and of lust for power met their match. . . . I should like to have it said of my second Administration that in it these forces met their master."[1] No American president has rivaled Roosevelt in his denunciation of what he called "economic royalists." He sought to "master" the "forces of selfishness" by making government master of every person's private financial destiny. Like today, the citizen who wanted to retain control over his own life was selfish, while the bureaucrat who wanted to seize power over the citizen was automatically presumed benevolent.

One of the most controversial New Deal policies was the seizure of citizens' gold.[2] During the Great Depression, several foreign nations repudiated their promises to redeem their currencies for gold. In 1933, when Roosevelt became president, the United States had the largest gold reserves of any nation in the world. He announced on March 8, 1933, a few days after taking office, that the gold standard was safe. But three days later, he issued an executive order forbidding gold payments by banks; Treasury

Secretary Henry Morgenthau, Jr., announced on March 11 that "the provision is aimed at those who continue to retain quantities of gold and thereby hinder the Government's plans for a restoration of public confidence." [3] Thus, according to Morgenthau, any limit on government power was bad for public confidence. And whatever confidence people might seek to achieve must be left in abject dependence on politicians' latest salvation scheme.

The ban on bank gold payments created widespread doubts about the Roosevelt administration's intentions. Ogden Mills, who had served as President Herbert Hoover's treasury secretary, observed that "it was not the maintenance of the gold standard that caused the banking panic of 1933 and the outflow of gold. . . . [I]t was the definite and growing fear that the new administration meant to do what they ultimately did-that is, abandon the gold standard." [4] People naturally sought to get rid of their paper currency and to put their savings into something with more secure value-gold.

Gold as Contraband

Fear of devaluation spurred a panic, which Roosevelt invoked to justify seizing people's gold. On April 5, 1933, Roosevelt commanded all citizens to surrender their gold to the government. No citizen was permitted to own more than $100 in gold coins, except for rare coins with special value for collectors. Morgenthau announced on the same day that "gold held in private hoards serves no useful purpose under present circumstances." [5] Gold was thus turned into the same type of contraband as Prohibition-banned rum. Roosevelt announced, "Many persons throughout the US. have hastened to turn in gold in their possession as an expression of their faith in the Government and as a result of their desire to be helpful in the emergency.

There are others, however, who have waited for the Government to issue a formal order for the return of gold in their possession." [6] To speak of the "return of gold" implied that government was the rightful owner of all the gold in the nation, and thus that no citizen had a right to possess the most respected store of value in history. Roosevelt assured the country: "The order is limited to the period of the emergency." But the order stayed on the books until 1974.

Roosevelt labeled anyone who did not surrender his gold a "hoarder." His executive order defined "hoarding" as "the withdrawal and withholding of gold coin, gold bullion or gold certificates from the recognized and customary channels of trade." [7] Actually, Roosevelt was not concerned with the gold being in the "customary channels of trade"; instead, he wanted government to possess all the gold. And the notion that people were "withholding" their gold merely because they did not rush to the nearest Federal Reserve bank to surrender it was political logic at its best.

Roosevelt, in a later note to his Public Papers, justified the order because it "served to prevent the accumulation of private gold hoards in the US." [8] Roosevelt used the same "hoarding" rhetoric against anyone who owned gold that Stalin used against Ukrainian peasants who sought to retain part of their wheat harvest to feed their families. But while Stalin sent execution squads to kill peasants who had a few bushels of grain hidden in their hovels, Roosevelt was kinder and gentler, seeking only ten-year prison sentences and $250,000 fines for any citizen who defied his edict and possessed more than five Double Eagle gold coins.

Roosevelt was hailed as a visionary and a savior for his repudiation of the government's gold commitment. Citizens who distrusted the government's currency management or integrity were branded as social enemies, and their gold was seized. And for what? So that the government could betray its promises and capture all the profit itself from the devaluation it planned. Shortly after Roosevelt banned private ownership of gold, he announced a devaluation of 59 percent in the gold value of the dollar. In other words, after Roosevelt seized the citizenry's gold, he proclaimed that the gold would henceforth be of much greater value in dollar terms.

Citizens who had desired to hold gold as a hedge against government inflation policies were completely vindicated. FDR's administration subsequently did everything possible to inflate prices, foolishly confident that a mere change in numerical prices would produce prosperity. Citizens had accepted a paper currency based on the government's pledge to redeem it in gold at $20 per ounce; then, when Roosevelt decided to default on that pledge, he also felt obliged to turn all citizens holding gold into criminals. Roosevelt stated that the ban on private ownership "was the first step also to that complete control of all monetary gold in the United States, which was essential in order to give the Government that element of freedom of action which was necessary as the very basis of its monetary goal and objective." [9] But the primary "freedom" government acquired was the freedom to default on its promises and to manipulate the lives of everyone depending on US. dollars in their daily transactions.

Curiously, FDR retained his denigrating tone toward so-called gold-hoarders even after he defaulted on the federal government's gold redemption promise. Even though people who distrusted politicians' promises were vindicated, they were still evil people because they had not obeyed FDR's demand to surrender their gold. In the moral world of the New Deal, justice consisted solely of blind obedience to political commands. FDR had absolutely no sense of embarrassment or shame after he defaulted on the federal government's gold promises-it was simply political business as usual.

Senator Carter Glass of Virginia, chairman of the Senate Finance Committee, denounced the gold seizure: "It's dishonor. This great government, strong in gold, is breaking its promises to pay gold to widows and orphans to whom it has sold government bonds....."[10]

Free to Inflate

The refusal to convert paper dollars into gold meant that the government was "free" to flood the country with paper money and sabotage the currency's value. The stability of the value of currency is one of the clearest measures of a government's trustworthiness. Before Roosevelt took office, Americans clearly recognized the moral implications of inflation. Vice President Calvin Coolidge had bluntly declared in 1922: "Inflation is repudiation." Inflation is a tax whereby government prints extra money to finance its deficit spending. The value of money is largely determined by the ratio of money to goods; if the quantity of money increases faster than the increase in the amount of goods, the result is an increase in the ratio of money to goods and an increase in prices. Thus, the government's printing presses devalue people's paychecks and effectively allow government to default on the value of its debt.

The threat of inflation was invoked in the early 1940s to justify imposing payroll tax withholding [11] (protecting people from their own paychecks) and in the 1970s to impose price controls over the entire economy. Apparently, politicians who decide to flood the money supply automatically become entitled to increase their coercion of their victims who hold increasingly worthless currency.

Since Roosevelt banned citizens from owning gold in 1933 and forced people to rely on the unbacked promises of politicians for the value of their currency, the dollar has lost about 93 percent of its purchasing power. [12] The collapse in the dollar's purchasing power severely disrupted the ability of scores of millions of Americans to plan their own lives and save for retirement. If someone proposed a law to give government the right to explicitly default by 2 to 3 percent a year on all its debts, the proposal would be widely denounced. Yet, this is what the government has been doing for decades. Though inflation has slowed since 1980, the purchasing power of the dollar has fallen by over 50 percent in subsequent years according to the government's own numbers (which slightly exaggerate the damage to the dollar), making a mockery of people's attempts to calculate and save for the future. A 1997 study by Congress's Joint Committee on Taxation found that because of how capital gains taxes are calculated, many citizens are forced to pay taxes on investment "gains" when in reality they have suffered losses due to the deterioration of purchasing power. [13]

Roosevelt's gold seizure was based on the doctrine that in order for government to save the people, it must be permitted to breach all the promises it made to the people. According to modem conventional wisdom, government has no obligation to do justice or treat any specific individual citizen fairly-instead, government's only duty is to achieve "social justice" or some other abstraction perfectly suited for evasion.

About the Author

James Bovard is the author of "Freedom in Chains: The Rise of the State and the Demise of the Citizen" (St. Martin's Press, 1999).

[1] *The Public Papers and Addresses of Franklin Roosevelt, 1936 (New York: Random House, 1938), pp. 232-33.*

[2] *Editor's note: See Richard Timberlake's article "Gold Policy in the 1930s," The Freeman, May 1999.*

[3] *Gustav Cassell, The Downfall of the Gold Standard (New York: Augustus Kelley, 1966 [1936]), pp. 118-19.*

[4] *Barry J. Eichengreen, Golden Fetters: The Gold Standard and the Great Depression (New York: Oxford University Press, 1992), p. 321.*

[5] *Cassell, p. 124,*

[6] *The Public Papers and Addresses of Franklin D. Roosevelt, The Year of Crisis, 1933 (New York: Random House, 1938), pp. 110-11.*

[8] *Ibid., p. 114.*

[9] *Ibid., p. 115.*

[10] *Benjamin Anderson, Economics and the Public Welfare (Indianapolis: Liberty Fund Press, 1979 11949]), p. 314.*

[11] *Charlotte Twight, "Evolution of Federal Income Tax Withholding," Cato Journal, Winter 1995. See http://www.cato.org/pubs/ journal/ cj 14n3-I.html.*

[12] *For information on the deterioration of the dollar's purchasing power, see the Web site of the U.S. Bureau of Labor Statistics at http:// www.bls.gov/cpihome.htm.*

[13] *Bruce Bartlett, "How Inflation Hikes the Capital Gains Bite," Washington Times, March 31, 1997.*

Gold Standards

Charles Curley

Many Free Market Advocates are familiar with the gold standard, and why a gold standard is preferable to a flat standard. But there are several different kinds of gold standards, each with its own characteristics and its own implications for the economy.

The earliest and simplest form of gold standard is trading for gold in the form of gold dust or gold bullion. There are no banks or money substitutes whatever, and the total money stock is simply the total amount of gold in the trading area. This form of gold standard requires no government intervention in the economy at all, and requires of the government only the prosecution of fraud, which is easy to prove since contracts (written or verbal) are defined in terms of a specified amount of gold in a specified form.

Gold for this purpose is constantly being provided by gold mines or foreign trade and refined into recognizable forms by known refiners. If the purchasing "power"* of money (gold) increases, then it will become profitable to mine or import more gold (by exporting more products). This will bring about an expansion of the gold stock, which, other things being equal, will reduce the purchasing "power" of money until the profitability of mining or importing gold is comparable to the profitability of other activity, and the marginal mines and importers will cease production.

* I put the term "power" in quotes to avoid confusion with political power, which purchasing "power" is not.

This is one example of how, with no government intervention, a commodity standard money tends to keep a constant purchasing "power" by a simple market mechanism, based on the profit motive of the people involved. Notice that neither gold miners nor anyone else are concerned with such things as the stock of money or other esoteric economic concepts, yet it is they who act to stabilize the purchasing "power" of money when it becomes necessary.

Primitive and inconvenient

This gold standard is rather primitive, as it requires the inconvenience of weighing out amounts of gold for each purchase, and the fact that one must carry one's gold around with him, an obvious temptation to muggers.

The solution to the first problem is to manufacture slugs of gold in uniform amounts with a uniform purity so that one can tell at a glance how much gold is in the slug. Since the gold content is known, the manufacturer can alloy the gold with other metals to harden the coin, thus reducing wear. The manufacturer's name and the weight of fine gold are stamped on the coin. A modern example is the Krugerrand, which is minted by the South African Chamber of Mines (all the government does is provide the dies). It carries the legend, "FYNGOUD 1 OZ. FINE GOLD" (in Afrikaans and English).

Because the gold is what is valued, and not the alloy or fancy designs on the two faces, the unit of weight of fine gold becomes identified with the coin. For example, the dollar was at one time defined as 1/20th of an ounce of gold simply because the United States coin of one ounce was labeled "20 Dollars."

Of course, there is always a possibility of fraud on the part of the minter, and the objection is usually raised at this point: "Why, we can't trust people to mint coins! That function has to be turned over to the government!"

We can trust private manufacturers to mint coins according to the market's specifications just as we can trust private firms to manufacture nuts and bolts to specification, or carry the mail. Advocates of the free market maintain that private enterprise can provide every other product or service better than the government can. Why not coins?

But the introduction of coins still leaves two problems: storage and convenience. The convenience problem is two-sided. In the case of large purchases, one must transport a lot of gold around to make the payment. One runs into the problems of transportation and security. Small purchases, say a piece of bubble gum, would require the availability of a coin small enough to pay for it or make change if a large coin is presented. This problem would be solved by the market by the use of a bimetallic system, as where gold and silver circulate side by side.

Bimetallism

Bimetallism here simply means that the market accepts either gold or silver as money. This is a decision that must be left to the market. It is like having two currencies. The idea of having two (or more) currencies is far more disturbing to Americans than to Europeans, who might have to deal in sterling one minute, Swiss francs the next, and then dollars. It simply requires that people express their prices in terms of both gold and silver, just as many European shops express their prices in both dollars and the local currency. The bimetallic system simply means that the monetary metal with the lower purchasing power per unit of mass would be used to make the smaller purchases, such as bubble gum.

Another innovation solves several problems. The introduction of warehouses for money solves, of course, the problem of safely storing one's money. The warehouse would store your gold for a fee and give you a receipt for the gold. It is still your gold, and the fact that it is in someone else's storehouse does not mean that title to the gold passes to him or that he has any other claim to the gold (except possibly to ensure payment of the storage fees). Because it is your gold, the warehouse has no more right to use it for any purpose than an employee in a furniture warehouse has to sit on your chair. Also, the warehouse must deliver your gold upon demand, just as the furniture warehouse must deliver your chair when you want it.

The receipts are usually in the form of bearer receipts, which means that the warehouse will deliver the gold to whoever presents the receipt for redemption. This carries with it the obvious implication: don't lose your receipts! But it also carries the implication that, instead of trading the physical gold, clients of warehouses can trade the receipts back and forth. But, still, as with the coins, the value is attributed to the gold, not the piece of paper.

A Modern Example

A modern example of the gold warehouse is the gold certificate offered by the Bank of Nova Scotia. Although the certificates are issued in ten-ounce lots with a minimum purchase of twenty ounces, the principle of the gold warehouse is maintained, as the Bank of Nova Scotia keeps on hand all the gold which its certificates represent. The storage fee is defined as 3¢ per hundred ounces per day, or $10.95 per year for up to one hundred ounces.

An alternative to issuing one or several receipts which would circulate in place of gold is to have the warehouse give the depositor a book of checks which he could use to make payments of exact amounts of gold, limited only by the availability of coins or bullion to make the exact amount of the check. (If the smallest amount of gold available is 5 grams, it does no good to write out a check for 9 grams, because no one makes small enough gold bars to pay the check.) This makes it easier to make purchases in that the buyer need only fill out the check for the exact amount of the purchase. However, the purchaser must not only establish the trustworthiness of his warehouse, but also whether he has enough gold in his account to cover the check.

Full Reserves

What I have described here is called 100 per cent reserve banking, which means that for every ounce worth of receipts outstanding, the warehouse has an ounce of gold in the vaults. The receipts are substitutions for rather than additions to the gold in the vault, and the money stock stays the same as gold flows into or out of the warehouse. The 100 per cent reserve banking system also differs from other bank systems in that the gold is considered to belong to the holder of the receipt, not to the bank or warehouse.

Because the warehouse operator is in the business of handling money, it is only natural that he should make a market for the use of it. When a warehouse operator matches up savers and borrowers so that the savers can earn interest on their savings, he becomes a banker. He facilitates this money market by accepting deposits of gold over a specified time and lending the money out over the same or a lesser period of time. He charges the borrower a higher rate of interest than he pays the depositor, the difference being the banker's profits. A modern example of this is the certificate of deposit, where the bank can pay you a higher interest rate than on a regular checking or savings account because it knows that you are going to leave the money on deposit for a specified period of time.

However, soon enough a banker will notice that most of the gold on deposit in his bank, even though in demand deposits, will be left in the bank for years, as the receipts are traded back and forth. If no one is going to redeem this gold, he reasons, why shouldn't I lend it out to someone else? Of course, the fact that he is lending out money that doesn't belong to him, that was entrusted to him, doesn't bother him; no one will find out, will they?

Even easier is to continue to hold the gold in his vault and instead lend out receipts for gold that doesn't exist. No one will find out; our banker won't lend out so much money that receipts brought for redemption will remove the entire gold stock from his vault. Of course, the fact that he is lending out gold that doesn't even exist doesn't bother him in the least, even if it is fraud.

Fractional Reserve

When the banker lends out the gold in his vaults, or lends out false receipts, he obviously no longer has enough gold in his bank to pay off the obligations of the bank. He has gone from 100 per cent reserves to fractional reserve banking. He also has created more circulating medium (money) than there was previously, but without the limiting device of the costs of mining or importing gold. It costs less than an ounce of gold to mine an ounce of gold, but, as more gold is mined than lost through wear, and as the purchasing "power" of money goes down, eventually the marginal mines find that it costs more than one ounce to mine one ounce of gold, and so they cease production. With pseudo-receipts, the limiting, cost of production is the cost of printing!

Thus, when a bank goes off 100 per cent reserves, its action results in more circulating media, which tends to lower the purchasing "power" of money. In other words, while 100 per cent reserve banking cannot be inflationary, fractional reserve banking must be.

Governments benefit from inflation. A very simple example is where politicians promise to "stimulate the economy" and proceed to inflate the currency in order to do so. Sometimes they are under the mercantilist mistake that more currency is the same thing as more wealth, so they encourage banks to create more currency. Obviously, in order to create more currency, the banker has to resort to fractional reserve banking. Usually, when the government is in on the deal, it will help out by giving banks a special status. The government simply removes the title to the gold from the holder of the receipt and gives the title to the bank. Notice that fractional reserve banking in all its variations requires this invasion of property rights, this intervention in the market.

At this point, the biggest thing that the bank has to fear is the possibility of a bank run, where all the depositors line up to retrieve their gold (that isn't all there). In order to avoid the temptation to create so much paper money that a bank run is precipitated, the government steps in, not to enforce the fraud laws, but to set reserve requirements, which specify what per cent of outstanding notes the bank must have in gold in its vaults. For example, if the government sets a reserve requirement of 25 per cent and a bank has $250,000 in outstanding currency, then the bank must have at least $62,500 in gold in its vaults.

The lower the reserve requirement, the more money the bank can create and lend out. If the government raises the reserve requirement, then banks may have to call in outstanding loans in order to meet the new requirements.

Debtors Gain

A government in debt (like any debtor) has much to gain from inflation. A rate of price increases of 10 per cent means that the government gains 10 per cent while the lender loses by that amount. As the federal government is the largest single debtor in the U.S., it obviously has much to gain by inflation: both in reduced value of the debt, and in having available newly created dollars which it can borrow without the politically objectionable side effect of higher interest rates.

One way to decrease the reserve requirements without running the risk of a bank run is to make it more difficult for people to redeem bank notes in gold. By raising the minimum lot for which one could trade his paper, banks make it harder for note holders to get gold. Thus, Britain, after World War land a great decrease in reserve requirements - changed the minimum amount of gold from a sovereign (a fraction of one ounce) to 400 ounces.

This restrictive gold standard is called a gold bullion standard, and stands in opposition to the original U.S. gold standard, where one could get gold for as little as $5, which was called a gold coin standard. The gold bullion standard allowed the Bank of England to continue with its wartime reserve requirements of 18 per cent instead of returning to the pre-war level of 52 per cent. This, in turn, meant that the British banking system did not have to deflate in order to return to the level of credit imposed by a 52 per cent reserve requirement.

Restricted Redemption

Another way to limit gold outflow is to limit the people to whom the bank will give tip the gold. The U.S. did this quite abruptly in 1933 by prohibiting Americans from owning gold, and hence, from turning in their paper for gold. This meant that only foreigners could trade their dollars for gold.

Although still nominally tied to gold, at this point the dollar was really a fiat currency; at any time the link between the dollar and gold could be severed, as we saw in August of 1971. In the late 1960's, it became apparent that Europeans were willing to buy all the gold that the U.S. would offer on the London gold market. Rather than deflate, the U.S. authorities ceased selling gold on the free market, and established the two-tier market in 1968. The free market price of the dollar soon moved down to 1/42nd of an ounce of gold, while central banks continued to trade gold at the old price of 1/35th of an ounce. Then, in 1971, even the central banks were banned from trading their dollars for gold. The U.S. had, for the first time since the 18th century, a completely fiat currency, in both the economic and legal sense.

It was during this period that the concept of a "price of gold" first came into use. When a currency is divorced from gold so that its purchasing "power" becomes different than that of the amount of gold which the currency originally was defined to be, then it can be said to be a fiat currency. It still may have ties to gold, such as the rather tenuous link between the dollar, the SDR, and gold from 1971 to 1973; but these are mere legalisms. As the fiat currency loses purchasing "power" relative to gold, then an ounce of gold will buy more and more units of the currency. This readjustment can be done occasionally and abruptly, via the mechanism of devaluations, or over a period of time via daily quotes on an organized private market such as the London Gold Market or the Commodity Exchange in New York. Thus, the monetary unit was divorced from gold in the eyes of the market as well as the government, and the dollar, for example, became defined as . . . well, a dollar, instead of 1/20th of an ounce of gold. Once this mental division is made, it is possible to talk of a "price of gold" just as one can talk of a "price of Swiss francs" or a "price of roast beef": each is a separate commodity from the unit of account -the (fiat) dollar.

Central Banking

During this century, the United States also moved away from free banking by modifying the reserves that banks could use for their deposits. Before the establishment of the Federal Reserve (in 1913), banks used gold, either bullion or coins, as reserves. However, with the establishment of the Fed, banks were allowed to deposit dollars with the Fed and count these deposits as reserves (still fractional).

The Fed learned rapidly how it could manipulate these reserves. Not only could it modify reserve requirements, but it could change the level of reserves in the banking system. The mechanism is very simple: the Fed buys an asset, any asset. To pay for it, the Fed writes out a check to the seller. The seller deposits the check in his bank, and the bank credits his account with the proper amount. Then, the bank presents the check to the Fed for collection. Instead of simply paying the bank so many dollars, the Fed credits the bank's reserve account with the Fed with the amount of the check. The bank's reserves are now expanded by the amount of the check, and the bank can now create and lend out additional dollars.

Any Debt Will Do

It is important to note in passing that the Fed can expand reserves by buying any asset. The most popular assets with the Fed are Treasury debts; and why not: they are buying the obligations of their parent organization, the U.S. government. But simply balancing the Federal budget will not deprive the Fed of assets to buy; simply balancing the budget will not stop inflation. After all, if the Fed couldn't get Treasurys, it could always buy New York Citys!

This system of expanding reserves means that the banking system can expand its reserves without regard to gold. Now, the Fed can inflate the money supply whenever anyone wants to go into debt, a not uncommon event! Even if the U.S. were to sell off all the gold in the Treasury stock, the Fed could continue to inflate, simply because someone would be willing to go into debt to buy that gold, or something else.

We have traced an evolution away from free banking toward the completely state-managed money system. Each step in between has been given a label, such as "gold exchange standard" or "gold bullion standard," each calculated to imply that the new setup was some form of gold standard. Even the Bretton Woods system was called a "gold-dollar standard" (not that the central banks even traded gold among themselves unless they had to - Gresham's Law applies to central bankers too).

Market Money or Political Money

The essence of the gold standard is that the gold in a bank's vaults regulates the credit that it can extend, and that the stock of money is regulated by the free market (specifically, the profitability or lack of profitability of gold mining), and not by the decisions of the bankers, especially the central bankers! Each step that was taken away from a 100 per cent reserve gold standard also made it both more necessary and easier to take the next step toward regulation. Each step also reinforced the idea that every time the banking system got into trouble, the government could bail it out, and do so by changing the banking system. Thus, later standards were gold standards only by virtue of a formal, legal link to gold. There was no commitment to gold, so whenever the banking system got itself into trouble, it was bailed out by the government-by another step away from gold.

Each step was supposed to make the banking system "more flexible," to make it easier to "meet the legitimate needs of business." But, as we have seen, each step has really had the effect of making it easier for the banking system to inflate. If we turn this around, we can see that each step was a step away from sound money, market controlled, toward money controlled by a government with a vested interest in inflation.

It is in the interest of the free market advocate to understand the different varieties of gold standards and mixed gold-fiat standards that have existed. This is the only way in which one can answer the many myths that surround money and banking. For example, careful study shows that it was not capitalism that failed in the 1930's, but central banking that failed in the 1920's.

About the Author

At the time of the original publication, Charles Curley was the author of The Coming Profit in Gold (Bantam), and was a founding member of the National Committee to Legalize Gold.

Reprinted with permission from The Freeman, a publication of The Foundation for Economic Education, Inc., June, 1975, Vol. 25, No. 6.

Closer Look at Gold

Charles E. Weber

When we Contemplate the gold coins from previous centuries we are painfully reminded to what extent modern man has lost his monetary freedom and hence an important aspect of his economic freedom. For thousands of years, with only relatively few and brief exceptions prior to 1915 (or 1934 in the case of the United States) nearly all nations in the main stream of human progress have enjoyed the advantages of the use of gold coinage as a monetary medium. Cowrie shells, stone wheels, rolls of bright bird feathers, salt, bronze ingots and the like were generally the monetary media of only the least advanced peoples.

Restraints on the use of gold as a monetary medium were rare in previous centuries, so rare, in fact, that we are tempted to speculate that many of the social and economic problems besetting the world in recent decades might not simply be concomitant phenomena of the decline of the public monetary use of gold, but even the results of this decline. In our own case, it is probably not a mere coincidence that since 1934, when the monetary use of gold was prohibited to U.S. citizens, the public debt has climbed to levels that could scarcely have been imagined forty years ago, the purchasing power of the national monetary unit has deteriorated so badly that this decline has become a major national problem, export trade has declined, the centers of large cities have been rotting at an accelerated pace and the problem of overpopulation has begun to threaten the very quality of life to which we had become accustomed.

Prior to 1934 the use of gold as a monetary medium had been deeply rooted in our economic and legal traditions. Undoubtedly as a reaction to the chaos caused by excessive issues of paper money[1] before and during the Revolution, the Constitution provided in Article 1, Section 10, that "No state shall . . . make any Thing but gold and silver Coin a Tender in Payment of Debts."[2] A handsome U.S. gold coinage was commenced in 1795 to supplement the foreign gold in circulation, which continued to have the status of legal tender until 1857 on the basis of laws of 1793, 1816, 1834 and 1843. It was this sort of legal precedent that was the basis for the monetary stability of the country (and probably its economic progress) down to recent years.

Fiat Money in France

There is an interesting parallel in French monetary history. When the revolutionary government of France at the end of the 18th century tried to substitute paper money (assignats) supposedly based on the value of confiscated church properties, economic chaos resulted.[3] Later on, Napoleon I saw the need of a reform to overcome the paralysis and reinstated the use of the precious metals. His introduction of the twenty franc piece (the "napoleon") in 1803 was an act of far-reaching consequences, as we shall see below. Russia had also tried paper money, likewise designated by a similar word, assignashii.[4]

Although a number of governments make every desperate attempt to suppress the monetary use of gold, faith in the sun metal as a store of value is deeply ingrained in the economic common sense of human beings all over the world. When I was in Russia in the summer of 1970, a young man explained to me that the old five rouble pieces struck on the standard used beginning with 1897 are now fetching about 90 paper roubles, nearly a typical month's wages in the present Soviet State. The grimly strict monetary laws and energetic propaganda of the Soviet State[5] had not been able to eradicate a desire for and a trust in gold. During and immediately after World War II many a family was able to avoid starvation by gradually giving up one gold piece after the other to purchase food that could otherwise not be obtained in economies paralyzed by war and postwar controls.

A Coin at Work

Let us contemplate a half eagle struck by the young United States in 1800. As in the case of the vast majority of gold coins struck in the world before 1800, there is also no designation of value or weight on this piece. Gold coins need no designation of value or legal tender status to function well. The piece we are contemplating is worn, so badly worn that its designs are only slightly above the level of the fields, but its weight is 8.50 grams, only about 3 per cent below its legal weight of 135 grains (8.748 grams).

Now let us reconstruct the tremendous economic task that this gold piece performed so well and so long. The wear on this piece would suggest that it was in circulation at least until the weight reduction of 1834 and perhaps quite a bit longer. If it changed hands on the average of just once a week over a period of 50 years, it changed hands more than 2,500 times and was thus involved in an exchange of more than $12,500. However, the really remarkable aspect of this performance lies in the fact that every time it changed its owner, the new owner was guaranteed a stable value as long as he wished to keep the piece. What were the costs of this remarkable performance? About 15 cents' worth of gold lost through wear and the very modest cost of striking the piece. To have printed paper money for this period of circulation would have approached or exceeded the minting and gold loss costs. Far more important, however, is the fact that the costs of the gold loss and minting were a very trivial consideration in relation to the social and economic benefits of the gold piece. Modern paper money, without a connection with the precious metals, simply cannot fulfill the traditional capacity of gold coinage to function both as a medium of exchange and a store of value.

Not only does gold coinage go back to the early days of the American Republic, but it covers some twenty-seven centuries of Western Civilization. It was, -in turn, antedated by an even earlier, specifically monetary use of gold, a use that can be readily documented. Thus, a mural painting from Thebes, Egypt, assigned to the reign of Thutmosis III, 1501 - 1447 B.C., shows the weighing of gold rings and holed disks.[6] Details of this painting reveal the status that gold had attained as a monetary medium. The weights on the balance pan are in the form of bovine heads and sheep! This illustrates the fact that a transition had been made from an economy in which cattle were used as exchange to one in which the precious metals had taken their place, but the tradition of the cattle exchange is preserved in the very shape of the weights. To mention a later parallel, the earlier Latin word for money, pecunia, developed from pecus, meaning "cattle." In the case of the Teutonic languages, the German word for cattle, Vieh, is a cognate of English fee.

American Indian civilizations never developed a gold coinage as did the Europeans, but gold was used as a medium of exchange in the form of quills filled with gold dust. Undoubtedly, too, the many pre-Columbian gold ornaments, often of considerable artistic merit, played some sort of monetary role.

Coinage in Ancient Greece

The very beginnings of Greek gold (or more specifically, electrum) coinage are nebulous. One type with two confronted lions' heads is actually inscribed "Alyas," a variant form of the name of King Alyattes, fourth of the Mernmad kings of Lydia, who reigned 610-561 B.C. Far more abundantly preserved, however, are the electrum pieces of various weights (1/12, 1/6 and 1/3 staters) bearing the head of a lion with a radiate knob on the forehead. The weights of these pieces are astonishingly consistent. Six specimens of the 1/3 stater preserved in the Boston Museum of Fine Arts have the narrow range of 4.66 grams to 4.71 grams, with fractional pieces in a close proportion.7 Other very important early series of electrum coins were those of Kyzikos in Mysia (started before 550 B.C.), Mytilene on the island of Lesbos (ca. 500 B.C. ff.) and Phokaia in Ionia (started before 500 B.C.). These early gold series consisted of electrum, a more or less natural mixture of gold and silver, such as was mined in what is now western Turkey. Later on, more sophisticated refining methods were used to prepare the planchets. The huge gold coinages of the kings of Macedonia, Philip 11 (359-336 B.C.) and Alexander the Great (336-323 B.C.), are notable for the fact that they consisted of nearly pure gold, with specific gravities ranging around 19 (pure gold: 19.3 times the weight-of water). By the time the autonomy of the Greek states had been extinguished by the expanding Roman Empire, no less than fifty of them had struck gold coins.

The Roman Republic and subsequently the Roman Empire had as a gold unit the aureus, which was first struck in quantity around 46 B.C. At that time it had a weight of 1/40 of a Roman pound (8.19 g). Its high purity persisted but its weight gradually sank over a period of nearly four centuries.

The Solidus

The next great gold series, the solidus, got its start in the early fourth century under Constantine the Great (reigned 306-337 A.D.) - The solidus was one of the most remarkable and enduring of all gold coins. Its weight and fineness were maintained with only occasional variations for over seven centuries, in spite of all the military, economic and political vicissitudes of the late Roman Empire and its continuation in the east (the "Byzantine" Empire). During this very long period the solidus had little competition in[7] the world except for the gold of the Islamic dynasties which originally started as imitations of the Byzan-tine solidus during the seventh century. The Ostrogoths in Italy also imitated the solidus in great quantities during the fifth and sixth centuries, but unlike the Islamic imitations, the Ostrogothic solidi bore the name and portraits of the Byzantine emperor and can be distinguished from the Byzantine pieces only by subtle stylistic differences. So familiar was the world with the solidus that we seldom find specimens with cuts to test the authenticity of the pieces; forgeries of them were evidently rare. Hoards of them have been found as far away as Scandinavia. Although we have no exact mint records from the Byzantine Empire, the mintage of the solidus was certainly enormous. As late as about 1950, common, worn solidi could be had for as little as about $12, not much more than twice their bullion value.[8]

After the decline of the solidus in the later medieval period it was supplanted by several important Italian, Hungarian and German series. Florence struck the florino d'oro (gold florin) beginning with the year 1252. It was imitated in a land with big gold mines, Hungary, in the 14th century and later. In Germany and the Netherlands, in turn, large quantities of florins were struck in the 15th and early 16th centuries, but they declined in weight and fineness when the German gold mines began to be so badly depleted that the gold became too dear in relation to the huge supplies of silver flowing from Saxony and Bohemia. (The first large-scale coinage of the predecessor of the silver dollar was done in Saxony, 1500 ff.) The Rhenish gold florin was struck in enormous quantities in such towns as Frankfurt, Cologne, Nuremberg and Utrecht. A quarter million of them were struck in 1418 in Frankfurt alone and Basel struck 126,020 during the years 1434-5.

The Gold Ducat

On 31 October, 1284, the Maggior Consiglio of Venice decided to mint the gold ducat, one of the most important gold coins of all times. It is still being struck from dies dated 1915 in the Vienna Mint nearly 700 years later. In Venice itself, the ducat was struck with the same design (St. Mark and Doge) down to the end of the 18th century. The ducat weight and fineness became a favorite in Germany, the Netherlands, Poland, Scandinavia and Russia. It was even crudely imitated as far away as India, where the Venetian originals were also in use.

England, France, Spain and Portugal had many gold coinages in the later middle ages, but they were of great variety. An outstandingly successful English coin of the late medieval period was the noble, which was imitated to some extent in the Netherlands, but the English and French kings changed their standards too often to establish gold coins of the great success and influence of the solidus and the ducat. The Spanish exploitation of the large deposits in Mexico, Bolivia and Peru resulted in the huge escudo coinage of the 16th to 19th centuries. Its multiple of eight is familiar to us as the doubloon.

As noted above, the gold coinage of the United States was started in 1795, with a modest weight decrease in 1834, after which U.S. gold coinage was continued for almost exactly a century on the same standard. About 3/4 of the enormous U.S. gold coinage was in the form of double eagles (1850 ff.).

The Latin Monetary Union

In France a new gold coinage was introduced in 1803 that continued to be of great importance until 1914. Denominations of 5, 10, 20, 40, 50 and 100 franc pieces were struck at various times but the most important was the 20 franc piece. The French standard was copied in Italy, Switzerland, Belgium, Spain, Greece, Serbia, Bulgaria, Romania and other lands, in some cases with different names. Some gold coinage on the franc standard continued even after World War 1, especially in Switzerland. In recent years the French government has struck considerable quantities of gold using dies with older dates. The prosperous German Empire struck large quantities of gold on the mark standard (18711915), while the huge English sovereign coinage (1816 ff.) still dominates the trade in coined gold.

India had a long tradition of monetary gold use before the establishment of the present Republic of India with its socialistic orientation and hence hostility to private ownership of gold. Gold coinage of the European type was introduced to India no later than the time when the Bactrian Empire struck gold in a quite Greek form and with Greek inscriptions (ca. 250 B.C. ff.). Later on there were other very important Indian gold series. The Kushan gold coins were fairly close imitations of the Roman aureus, many hoards of which have also been found in India. The very abundant Kushan gold coinage was at first of high purity, like the Roman aureus, and it is even assumed that the planchets for it were prepared from remelted Roman gold. During the first and second centuries the Roman Empire had a severe balance of trade problem with India because of the commerce in spices, gems and other Indian goods desired by the luxury-loving Romans.

Debasement in India

With the decline of the Kushan Empire its gold coinage became severely debased, especially after about 200 A.D. After about 320 A.D. the Gupta kings also continued gold coinage in important quantities. After the decline of the Gupta realm, i.e., after about 450 A.D., a number of Hindu dynasties continued gold coinage. The famous uninscribed and enigmatic elephant pagodas of perhaps about 1300 and later are now believed to be the private products of Indian goldsmiths. In the north the Islamic rulers (the Sultans of Delhi and subsequently the Mughal Emperors) struck gold in large quantities. In the south, the Hindu Vijayanagar Empire struck large amounts of a very neat gold coinage between 1377 A.D. and the disastrous Battle of Tallikota in 1565. Beginning with the 16th century, various European powers struck gold series for their territories in India; the Portuguese, the Dutch, the French, the Danes and especially the British, who first imitated the trusted gold coinage of the moribund Mughal Empire before striking gold in the European style.

In Japan, which has gold mines that have been worked since medieval times, gold was used in the form of oval plates punched with various devices. During the 19th century base gold rectangles were produced in considerable quantities. Just as the Meiji Era brought so many other changes to Japan, its earliest years saw the introduction of a very beautiful gold coinage of occidental style based on the U.S. gold denominations. So highly prized are 20 yen pieces of 1870 (46,139 struck) that they fetch over one million yen today. With the exception of a few gold issues in this century, China has virtually no tradition of the coining of gold, although it has been prized for artistic uses for many centuries in China.

3000 Years of Gold

I have surveyed the history of gold coinage in some detail here in order to show what a great economic role it has played in nearly every civilization (with the notable exception of the Chinese), European traditions of the monetary use of gold can be traced back for nearly three millenia in the form of gold coins alone.

The decline of gold coinage we have witnessed during the last three to five decades[9] thus represents a radical departure in monetary affairs. The coining of gold had hitherto been interrupted only sporadically by attempts to substitute other media for the precious metals.

It is undeniably true that many modern economists harbor a strong bias against the monetary use of gold. This bias is by no means difficult to explain, since these economists are the ones who see the most important role for themselves in governments which intervene strongly in the economy. Gold strongly restricts governmental intervention in the economy and the redistribution of wealth from the productive to the non-productive components of the population. Perhaps to some extent, too, the bias against the monetary use of gold is simply based on ignorance about the present and past monetary roles of gold. After all, a new generation has come onto the scene since 1934.

We appreciate the role of gold as an honest, constructive monetary medium when we consider the nature of its enemies. Keynes, whom Lenin lauded before the Second Congress of the Communist International, considered gold a barbarous relic. Typically, the people who are shouting most loudly that gold is a barbarous relic are the very ones who are most adamant in their demands to suppress the monetary use of gold by force. (Who, really, are the barbarians?) These "experts" must know full well just how powerful gold is in spite of their public denials that it should play a role in the monetary system and in spite of their claims that it is worthless except for filling teeth and the like.

Private Coinage

When governments have refused or have been unable to strike gold coins in sufficient quantities for commerce, private persons have provided gold coins in many instances. We need only think of the many private gold coinages in the United States alone: the Bechtler gold pieces struck in North Carolina in the 1830s and later, in addition to the massive amounts of gold struck privately in California in the 1850s and later. There have also been many private gold series in India and Germany, for example. A large private striking of gold on the ducat standard has taken place in Germany during the last two decades. In addition, many forgeries of well-known gold types with full or nearly full weight and fineness have been made in large quantities in recent decades. The American double eagle, the British sovereign and the 20 franc piece have been favorite forms of the counterfeiters, whose activities have flourished on a vast scale in recent years because of the need for gold coinage and the failure of public mints to perform their traditional duties of providing gold in convenient form.

Because of the strong biases of many economists against the monetary use of gold, a number of myths and erroneous conceptions have grown up about gold coinage. Even some libertarian economists are lacking in sufficient knowledge about the history of gold coinage to refute the nonsense that is often deliberately propagated.

It is an error to assume that all gold coinages were constantly being eroded in value by debasement and weight reductions. Indeed, the really important gold series were struck over long periods of time, in some instances for many centuries, without substantial reductions. One need only think of the solidus, the ducat, the escudo and the vast gold coinages of the nineteenth century; the sovereign, the double eagle and the napoleon.

It is also an error to assume that the frauds committed in connection with gold coins were of very great importance. Sometimes coins were filed or sweated (friction in bags in which the gold dust was collected) and sometimes test cuts were made by which a small amount of gold was removed. However, such frauds could readily be detected by gold scales. Forgeries existed and there were printed descriptions of them as early as the 15th century. Still, such frauds are quite insignificant compared to the vast frauds carried out in connection with paper money, which is cheaper to counterfeit than gold coins. Of vastly greater importance, of course, is the fraud carried out against productive citizens by governments themselves which refuse to coin precious metals and keep issuing ever greater quantities of paper money.

It is still another error to assume that gold is the ally only of the wealthy. In this age of complicated tax laws and deceptive monetary policies it is the wealthy who can afford the best advice on taxes and investments. For the saver of modest means, a little hoard of gold and silver has often proved to be the best protection against confiscation of his savings by devaluations of currency.

There's Plenty of Gold

The argument that there is "no longer enough gold for monetary purposes" is one of the more absurd arguments that has been made against the return to the monetary use of gold. The United States could start minting gold again within the very short time required to prepare the dies. Plenty of gold could be delivered to the mints from the mines now kept idle by governmental restrictions. Any seigniorage charged should not exceed the actual minting costs. As to the relation of the new gold coins to the huge heaps of paper money now in circulation, the problem could be easily circumvented simply by omitting any designation of value on the coins and employing the familiar weights and fineness of the quarter eagles, half eagles, eagles and double eagles. The double eagles, for example, might bear the inscription "516 GRAINS, 900 FINE" instead of the erstwhile "TWENTY DOLLARS." As in previous generations, the deliverers of gold to be minted would be charged a small fee for minting costs and the gold pieces would be theirs to keep or put into commerce.

Striking gold coins without any designations of value on them is a procedure that was not only used in previous centuries, but also in recent decades. Consider the following examples: Beginning in 1921, Mexico had struck gold pieces somewhat larger than the U.S. double eagle. The Mexican pieces are known as the "centenario" because they originally commemorated the centennial of the Republic. For years these pieces were struck in large quantities with the designation of 50 Pesos. By 1943, however, the designation had become meaningless because of the considerable depreciation of the value of the Mexican paper and silver currency. In 1943 the centenario appeared without the usual inscription of 50 Pesos but with an inscription describing the weight and fineness, the really important factors. There are many variations on the procedure. Great Britain, for example, struck over 30 million sovereigns between 1957 and 1966 for overseas trade. These continued to bear no designation of value, just as all modern sovereigns (since 1816) had borne none.

Market Sets the Value

If the government were to resume the striking of gold pieces, as it should without delay, it would be easy to determine what designation of value, if any, were to be put on them after supply and demand had established a price in terms of other media. For purely monetary purposes, however, no designation of value would really be necessary, since gold coins need no legal tender status to work well, both as a medium of exchange and as a store of value.

The lessons of monetary history are clear. Without the resumption of gold coinage or at least a free commerce in all of the precious metals, including especially gold, inflation will go on and on and on. Even just the tolerance of a free gold market would inhibit inflation by providing a constant gauge of the value of other monetary media.

Those being hurt by inflation should bear the following in mind: The reason that governments with a redistributive economic philosophy frown on gold coins is because of the fact that inflation is a big aid if not, indeed, an essential factor in the redistributive process. If those persons in government circles who are talking about "fighting inflation" were at all sincere, they would immediately remove all restrictions on the mining and monetary use of gold and resume a governmental function which had been taken for granted for literally thousands of years in western thought, the striking of gold coins with an established weight and fineness.

Those being hurt by inflation have a powerful weapon at their disposal if they would only realize it and act accordingly. They could refuse to buy all bonds, public or private, that did not contain gold clauses. While it is true that gold obligations have been repudiated in the past,[10] the constant demand for gold obligations would undoubtedly have an influence on national monetary policies. Restoration of the right to own gold and make contracts in terms of gold would be a major step toward restoration of the basic principle of economic freedom, a freedom no less sacred than other freedoms. The restoration of our traditional rights with regard to gold should be vigorously supported by all those who prize economic freedom and abhor the emptiness, stagnation, decay and oppression of the omnipotent socialistic state.

About the Author

Dr. Charles E. Weber received his Ph.D. from the University of Cincinnati in 1954 on the basis of a dissertation on the incunabula (books printed prior to 1501 A.D.) in the German language. After military service in World War II, at times as a member of intelligence unit!, he resumed his education and started his teaching career at the University of Missouri and the University of Tulsa, at the time of this publication, he had been teaching since 1956 except for four years at Louisiana State University (1962-1966).

Dr. Weber is the author of numerous articles on literature, history and monetary questions.

End Notes

[1] For a thorough, lavishly illustrated history of the paper money issues of our land from 1690 to 1789 see the brilliant volume by Eric P. Newman, The Early Paper Money of America. Racine, 1967.

[2] In defending this provision, James Madison (The Federalist Papers, No. 10) speaks of "A rage for paper money, for an abolition of debts, for an equal division of property, or for any other improper or wicked project. . . ." In No. 44 he continues in the same vein: ". . . the pestilent effects of paper money on the necessary confidence between man and man, on the necessary confidence in the public councils, on the industry and morals of the people, and on the character of republican government . . ."

[3] For details, see Andrew D. White, Fiat Money Inflation in France (Irvington, N. Y.: Foundation for Economic Education).

[4] *See the well illustrated volume on Russian monetary history by I. G. Spasskii. Russkaia Monetnaia Siatema, "Aurora" Press, Leningrad, 1970, p. 201.*

[5] *Strange to say, during the early years of the Soviet State, gold coins were struck with the weights of the older ten-rouble pieces struck as late as 1911. The Soviet gold pieces were dated 1923 and bore the emblem of the State and a sowing peasant. There is evidence that these pieces were struck in very large quantities, but today they are very scarce. Doubtless the bulk of them were remelted.*

[6] *For a reproduction of this painting, see Heinrich Quiring, Gegchichte des Goldes / Die Goldenen Zeitaiter in ihrer kulturellen und wirtschaftlichen Bedeutung. Ferdinand Enke Verlag, Stuttgart, 1948, page 48. This book, by the way, is an excellent source of information on the history of the mining, refining and use of gold.*

[7] *An excellent source for the metrological aspects of the earliest electrum coinage, including the specific gravities of many specimens, is the catalogue of the holdings of the Boston Museum of Fine Arts published by Agnes Brett in 1955.*

[8] *To illustrate the constancy of the solidus, specimens in the author's collection weigh as follows: A solidus struck in Milan under Honorius (395-423A.D.) weighs 4.47 grams with a specific gravity of about 18. A lightly circulated specimen Of Constantine WIT (1025—1028) with an inspiring portrait of Christ weighs 4.37 grams with a specific gravity of a bit less than 19, nearly pure gold. In the subsequent decades the weight and fineness of the solidus declined sharply, but Byzantine gold coinage persisted into the 14th century. For a detailed analysis of the debasement of the solidus in the eleventh century, see Byzantinische Zeit-schrift, 1954, pp. 379-394.*

[9] *The coining of gold has by no means ceased altogether, even in the case of governmental mints, During the last 10 to 15 years or so the following governments have struck gold in quantity: Austria, Republic of China, Dominican Republic, Egypt, France, Great Britain,*

Katanga, Mexico, Persia, Peru, South Africa, Spain and Turkey. In some cases older dies were used. Many other lands have also struck gold in token quantities.

[10] *But not without a loss of face. The refusal of the United States to redeem gold bonds after 1934 was perhaps the greatest breach of faith that had been committed by it as of then. The exact wording of these bonds is significant. Gold bonds dated May 9, 1918, for example, contain the following clause: "The principal and interest hereof are payable in United States gold coin of the present standard of value." Although the bankruptcy of an individual may be, in a technical legal sense, different from the bankruptcy of a nation, the failure to redeem national obligations in precious metals has always been an act parallel to the bankruptcy or dishonesty of an individual.*

Reprinted with permission from The Freeman, a publication of The Foundation for Economic Education, Inc., September, 1972, Vol. 22, No. 9.

Gold Has Risen - But Remains the Same

Donald McLaughlin

Not very long before his untimely death, Jacques Rueff in his fluent but slightly accented English commented that further debates on the status of gold in the monetary system seemed hardly necessary for "events were taking over." And indeed they have.

With surprisingly little fanfare, gold is maintaining its firm place in the world's reserves where it commands a respect far greater than any of the fiat currencies that pass for money these days. That this could happen in spite of the persistent anti-gold position of successive United States Administrations over more than four decades still further emphasizes its durability as money and the firm faith all manner of men have in it-apart from those who rule in Washington and bankers whose skill is largely in manipulation of the technicalities of increasingly complex instruments of credit.

The long record of human history surely reveals that when money, whether in the form of precious metal or credit, is debased and abused, a nation or even the entire world suffers. Today we are in a period of such misbehavior and mismanagement but the persistent strength of gold even under these trying conditions offers hope that, if it is used wisely and effectively, order can eventually be restored.

The principle currently known as Gresham's Law has been recognized for tens of centuries. It is as sound today as it was when Aristophanes used it in a metaphor to illustrate how good men were driven from public life in Athens in the same way that untrustworthy money forced better money out of circulation. At about the same time, Aristotle stated the concept more logically perhaps, but less poetically. Today, the principle is well understood in most high circles in Europe. In 1973, Milton Gilbert noted that gold remained unused in the vaults of the central banks-but not unloved. In America, unfortunately, the money managers and politicians seem less familiar with the classics.

Since then, eighteen governments (but not the United States) are valuing their official gold stocks closer to market prices - or more rationally expressed are putting the currencies they hold in a realistic ratio to gold. Furthermore, by utilizing gold at a market-related rate, the recently created European Monetary System has provided the Common Market countries with a mechanism for employing their gold reserves effectively in foreign exchange transactions. These wise moves tend to reduce the discrepancies that tend to immobilize gold in response to Aristophanes' or Gresham's Law, even though they do not remove all fears arising from the continued depreciation of fiat money.

According to our official policy, gold has now been demonetized and henceforth fiat currencies and credit instruments will be relied upon exclusively to perform the services expected from money. Their most distinctive quality unfortunately appears to be a tendency to decline in purchasing power, a very troublesome defect in anything that claims to be money.

"Paper Gold"

To overcome the restrictions imposed by national sovereignty and political borders, a strange device known as Special Drawing Rights was created by the International Monetary Fund, at first vaguely attached to gold and now defined in terms of a "basket" of currencies, all of which are depreciating in real value though at different rates. In essence, the SDRs were an attempt to create an international form of fiat money. For a time, their enthusiastic supporters even referred to them as "paper gold." So far, their acceptance even under duress has been restrained, to put it mildly.

Even though "demonetized" by the dictum of the United States, nearly a billion troy ounces of gold are still firmly held in the official reserves of the western nations, rather a substantial amount to declare was no longer legal money. This obvious preference for gold should be rather disquieting for those who regard Gresham's Law as obsolete.

A monetary system based exclusively on credit possibly could be made to function, if managed by a small group of knowledgeable men of intelligence and integrity, with complete political independence and power, as well as mastery of the technical intricacies of money and finance and unprejudiced understanding of both national and international conditions that influence policies. Until such paragons can be brought into existence, however, it will be safer to retain the discipline of gold as an element of the monetary system than to expect that those who manage money based on credit and on government fiat will do so with sufficient skill that it will in time attain the confidence now commanded by gold. From the record of centuries this can hardly be regarded as even a forlorn hope.

Significant Experiments

In the natural sciences, ideas and hypotheses are tested by controlled experiments and confirmed or rejected by their outcome. In the social sciences such definitive tests are rarely possible. But with regard to gold's place in the monetary system there have been episodes that have provided results of unusually positive sort.

The first that should have been regarded as a significant experiment was the effort of several governments at the instigation of the United States 22 years ago to maintain the official price of gold at $35 per ounce by making gold available at this rate on the London market to all who desired to purchase it. It was a costly experiment. After several billion dollars had been spent with little effect, except to transfer gold into hands eager to accept it at a bargain price, the drain on gold reserves soon became too apparent and excessive to be tolerated and the sales were abandoned close to the Ides of March in 1968, with self-serving explanations that the mission had been accomplished. It was accompanied by the abrupt announcement that sales and purchases of gold by the participating governments would be discontinued at the official rate except between Central Banks.

The restrictions on ownership of gold were not repealed but miners and others with gold to sell were permitted to do so on the market to specifically authorized purchasers for whatever price their metal might command. In spite of predictions by several prominent economists and politicians that without the support of the dollar the gold price would sink to much lower levels, this didn't happen. After a short period of little change, the price started to rise, and this trend has continued with the usual market swings but with each new peak rising above the last. The results of this experiment alone should have been accepted as proof that the price of gold can not be tied to an unconvertible currency, subject to manipulations that cause it to depreciate in value.

A second test with equally decisive results occurred during the international financial turmoil in 1971 that led to the closing of the "gold window" on August 15th, when the United States Administration announced that it would (or could) no longer redeem dollars held by Central Banks in gold at the official price which by that time had been raised from Roosevelt's $35 an ounce to the strangely precise figure of $42.22 per ounce. The magnitude of claims in dollars had for some time made it apparent that the pledge to honor them in such terms had become impossible to meet. In effect, the United States admitted bankruptcy, as far as its obligation was concerned to redeem such dollars in gold at the official rate. Again it was made clear except to those whose anti-gold fixation made them blind to realities that a fiat dollar can not control the worth of gold.

The third experiment was the attempt to check the rising price of gold on the market and the weakness of the dollar that it revealed by substantial sales of gold from the reserves of the United States Treasury and the gold held by the International Monetary Fund. Whatever those who initiated this policy had in mind, it is unlikely that they anticipated or desired that the market price of gold would rise in spite of the large quantities they disposed of.

Furthermore, in the course of these sales, the Central Banks of Europe have not reduced their stocks of gold and indeed have firmly held the gold returned to them by the IMF which hardly seems in accordance with the decision, sponsored by the United States, that gold had been demonetized. Even a number of the Developing Countries have preferred to accept their allotment of the IMF sales in gold rather than in the paper in which the so-called aid would have presumably been paid to them.

In the natural sciences, when the outcome of a series of experiments is so definite, even the most ardent advocates of the ideas being tested usually accept them as conclusive. Unfortunately, the anti-gold group in power in Washington continues to ignore their clear message.

An Encouraging Sign

Restoration of the gold standard, which would require redefinition of the major currencies in terms of gold and establishment of unrestricted convertibility at new fixed rates, hardly seems attainable until the abuses of credit and the increasing worldwide inflation have been corrected and ended. It is still an objective worth striving for but to achieve it would require more drastic and disciplined action than our electorate and our politicians seeking reelection are likely to accept in the foreseeable future.

Even though restoration of the gold standard for the time being may be ruled out, a new monetary system appears to be evolving in which gold will continue to have an important place and be a strong and stabilizing element. Progress toward this end is revealed, not only by the firm retention of gold stocks by the major reserve banks-with the exception of the ill—considered sales by the U.S. Treasury and its sycophant, the IMF-but also by the removal of restrictions on ownership of gold by citizens and the issuance by many nations of gold coins whose worth is primarily determined by their weight in gold. Among them, the one-ounce Krugerrand, various handsome Mexican coins with gold content stated in metric units, and new coins struck from old dies such as the Austrian Krona are notable examples. The designations in national currency units that some still bear are obviously meaningless. The principal contribution by the issuing government is its seal that justifies confidence that the gold content is as stated.

A timely step that would simplify and create better order, as well as strengthen the function of gold in the evolving monetary system, would be the creation and dissemination of a coin of uniform gold content, fineness and size that could become a standard by which other monetary devices could be measured.

A Coin of Uniform Weight

With one gram of gold adopted as the basic unit, a coin containing 10 grams of gold (0.322 ounces troy), in the 90% alloy with copper commonly used in coinage to provide hardness, would be a convenient size, slightly larger than the old American five-dollar gold coin or the British sovereign.

The acceptance of such a golden unit would probably be facilitated if the coins were minted by each of the major nations and their authenticity established by them. Uniformity in design would not be necessary. Their essential quality would be the common gold content. Competition in beauty and esthetic appeal would have much to commend it.

If an appropriate name for such 10 gram gold coins could be found that would be easily comprehended internationally, so much the better, but if not, there would be no harm in each nation using a term based on some aspect of the design in which it took pride.

The unit of measurement, however, should be one gram of gold which could be abbreviated as 1 gin Au, a designation that would be understood and translated into any language in this age of common scientific nomenclature. The 10 gm Au coin which could be acquired and handled would give the unit a tangible reality. This is a quality that Special Drawing Rights can never acquire, in spite of the presumption of their creators in calling them "paper gold."

Leave It to the Market

The rigid discipline of the gold standard, however, need not be imposed until desired. No tie need exist between any national fiat currency and the golden units. Any country would be completely free to indulge in whatever political, social or economic policies (or nonsense) it desired. The only restraint imposed by the gold in the reserves and the golden coins would be the effect on the market price of the currencies expressed in grams of gold. The objectionable term "the price of gold" could be abandoned, with currencies, as well as commodities and services, priced on the market in a unit containing a specific weight of gold. The plethora of quotations of currencies - dollars, marks, francs, yen, sovereigns, and the like expressed in each other, all variables measured by other independent and sometimes erratic variables-could be eventually abandoned. It would do no harm to continue such exchange quotations as long as the momentum of tradition required. But they should be accompanied by quotations in the proposed gold units, which would reveal the status of each national currency in one common standard.

Abuses of credit and excesses in creation of fiat currencies based on debt could hardly be concealed, for they would be promptly revealed in the price of the paper in gold. The economy obviously needs both elements-credit and stable money-but with gold effectively utilized in the monetary system a badly needed base would be provided upon which deficits, changes in quantity of fiat money and inflation, among other evils of the times, could be clearly revealed.

The Individual's Choice

The individual should of course have the privilege of acquiring the golden coins at rates determined by the market price of the currency he possessed. The denial of such a freedom by any government would in all probability be immediately and unfavorably reflected in the price of the currency.

The right to buy gold - especially coins - -actually puts into the hands of anyone desiring to do so, a very special commodity that has long possessed the essential qualities of money, viz., a medium of exchange, a means of measuring the relative value of other commodities and services, and a safe way to store wealth. The latter quality is not possessed today by any national currency.

The existence of a dominant gold coin-such as the one proposed, containing 10 grams of gold-would provide a simple constant, so to speak, against which all currencies could be measured with ease and confidence. It would, of course, not be a constant of value in the strict sense the term is used in mathematics and the physical sciences, but it would at least stand for a fixed quantity of gold. No commodity - not even gold - an claim to be invariable in worth and to provide an unchanging base for measurement of values of materials and services, but over the centuries gold has come nearest to doing this, as Roy Jastram has so well demonstrated in his recent book, The Golden Constant: The English and American Experience, 1560-1976 (John Wiley & Sons, Inc., 1977).

Three years ago, the title of a speech I gave at an annual gathering in a redwood grove in California was "The Resurrection of Gold Without Benefit of Clergy." Since then, in spite of the high priests in the Treasury and elsewhere in the government, Gold Has Risen as the dollar and other fiat currencies have deteriorated, and yet its worth, expressed in the cost in gold of a good dinner, a suit of clothes, a haircut or even a barrel of oil has not changed much. The Resurrection of Gold should now be regarded as demonstrated and as an important advance toward a sounder monetary system, with clear distinction between the status of money based on the relatively stable worth of the traditional monetary commodity - gold-and the variable national currencies that represent nothing more than credit in one form or another.

If this is coming about without formal conferences and long debates, so much the better. The open market even for currencies is a masterful device and one that is essential for economic freedom. It will continue to prevail and exert its influence even over the value of unconvertible currencies. With the variety of trustworthy coins now available, gold is already gaining more and more recognition as money in which currencies can be measured, and if a gold coin of established quality gains wide acceptance, the monetary system will be approaching a status in which there will be far better hope of attaining stability than has existed since World War II.

Flat Money Rejected

How the present uncertainties will end is hard to predict. In the last few months, the market "price" of gold has risen at an unexpectedly rapid rate. There are undoubtedly some undesirable factors involved, such as excessive transactions in gold futures, but by and large the accelerating rate at which gold has risen is to a much greater extent a result of the growing concern about the domestic economy and the deteriorating international situation, not to mention the persistence of deficit financing and the resulting unavoidable inflation. If the price of currencies were quoted in units of gold rather than the other way around, the instability attributed to gold by some of its detractors would be more clearly revealed as weaknesses in the artificial devices we now must use as money.

I do recall, however, that a few years ago when I was asked in a radio interview how high the price of gold would go, I replied that it had approached infinity in German marks in 1923. That need not and should not happen in America but with a few more years of persistent deficits and unwillingness to forgo extravagances in our way of life, it is a possibility that should not be lightly dismissed.

Stop Deficit Spending and Monetization of Debt

The first essential step to prevent such a disaster is to keep expenditures by the government within its income and to end monetization of debt. The second even more serious need is to find the least painful means of dealing with the tremendous and still mounting debt - domestic and international- that has now reached magnitudes that make its retirement by conventional means practically impossible. Reduction by default and/or by inflation are unfortunately much easier. Repudiation of debt in a more dramatic way would be the substitution of a new dollar for a number of existing dollars. Unfortunately this procedure is not without precedent. In 1926-28 Poincaré and in 1958 Charles de Gaulle created new francs for the then current francs that became known as "ancien francs." The creation of the Deutsche Mark is another example. These procedures were drastic though probably unavoidable. Such moves, however, in general are likely to be a mixture of good and evil-probably more of the latter than the former. But, if a country is forced to "bite the bullet" to correct past mistakes and excesses, liquidation of excessive debt by payment of a small fraction in sound money may not be the worst way and might even be the best way if the new currency - or the new dollar or whatever it might be - were made convertible into gold, when a durable rate could be established.

None of these disturbing developments is inevitable, but unless the American people and their leaders who are dependent on their votes have the will to put our house in order and accept the austerity that must be faced, events will indeed take over-and they are not likely to be pleasant.

About the Author

At the time of the original publication, Dr. Donald H. McLaughlin, mining geologist and engineer, formerly served as president and continued as a director and chairman of the executive committee of Homestake Mining Company.

Reprinted with permission from The Freeman, a publication of The Foundation for Economic Education, Inc., May 1980, Vol. 30, No. 5.

Gold Is Legal, But.....

Robert G. Anderson

TODAY, as was true 42 years ago, the American people once again have freedom to own as much gold as they choose. Devotees of the free market have viewed this development with pleasure, for they have had little cause to rejoice during these many years of steady erosion of individual liberty. Socialistic governmental intervention has steadily expanded since the denial of our right to own gold.

The restoration of legal gold ownership by individuals is certainly a reversal of this ominous trend of government omnipotence. It has been heralded as a sign of change in the course of statism. Upon closer scrutiny, however, such optimism may be questioned, for there is a marked distinction between conditions then and now.

What has been restored, and what was lost 42 years ago, are not the same. Prior to April 5, 1933, gold was money. Individuals used gold daily as their medium of exchange for goods or services at the rate of $20.67 an ounce of gold. It is true that the payment was rarely made in gold bullion, but the gold certificates or gold coins in use represented bullion. Gold was legal tender, along with the coins and currency of the Treasury and Federal Reserve Banks. Upon demand, anyone could surrender his paper money and receive gold bullion.

The legalization of gold ownership has not restored it as our medium of exchange-money. The statist legal tender laws (in conjunction with Gresham's Law) continue to force the fiat paper money of government upon us. The use of gold as money is still forbidden. Any attempt to use or demand gold payment for goods or services remains illegal. The absolute governmental monopoly of fiat money continues to be protected by law against competition from gold.

Calling in the Gold

The evolution of this government monopoly of money began with a Proclamation of President Roosevelt on April 5, 1933; under enabling legislation passed a month earlier, the destruction of gold as money commenced:

All persons are hereby required to deliver on or before May 1, 1933 ... all gold coin, gold bullion, and gold certificates now owned by them or coming into their ownership on or before April 28, 1933.... Until otherwise ordered any person becoming the owner of any gold coin, gold bullion, or gold certificates after April 28, 1933, shall, within three days after receipt thereof, deliver the same ... upon receipt of gold coin, gold bullion, or gold certificates delivered to it.... The Federal Reserve Bank or member bank will pay therefor an equivalent amount of any other form of coin or currency coined or issued under the laws of the United States.

This order called for the surrender of private gold holdings. Individuals, many believing it was merely a temporary action arising out of the "national emergency" of the great depression, obediently exchanged their gold for paper money.

The surrender of gold coins for paper money is understandable, inasmuch as gold could no longer be used as a medium of exchange. Individuals needed money to transact their exchanges. Since the exchange value of money at the time was greater than the commodity value of the gold content in the coins, people generally did not resist exchanging their gold for the remaining medium of exchange paper money.

But the government wanted to make sure of its money monopoly position. It wanted all the gold, and in furtherance of that end, President Roosevelt issued another Proclamation on August 28, 1933:

After 30 days from the date of this order no person shall hold in his possession or retain any interest, legal or equitable, in any gold coin, gold bullion, or gold certificates situated in the United States and owned by any person subject to the jurisdiction of the United States, except under license therefor issued pursuant to this Executive order....

While nominal holdings of gold were exempted from these edicts, any subsequent use of or holding of gold was under the direct control of government. Gold ownership was now illegal except under Treasury license and scrutiny.

It only remained to establish penalties for any violation to these edicts. This came in short order as a part of the Gold Reserve Act, January 30, 1934:

Any gold withheld, acquired, transported, melted or treated, imported, exported, or earmarked or held in custody, in violation of this Act ... shall be forfeited to the United States ... and in addition any person failing to comply with the provisions of this Act or of any such regulations or licenses, shall be subject to a penalty equal to twice the value of the gold in respect of which such failure occurred.

To all intent and purpose, the medium of exchange was now an irredeemable paper currency. Certain legal relationships prevailed between gold and money, but convertibility by United States citizens was ended. The only remaining convertibility was with foreign holders of our dollars. In time, even these provisions would disappear.

The Gold Reserve Act of 1934 transferred all the gold in the United States into the hands of the Treasury. The Federal Reserve Banks were issued "gold certificates" by the Treasury in exchange for their gold. It was cynically observed that "These are not certificates that you can get gold. These are certificates that gold has been taken away from you." [1]

Gold Repriced at $35

The abandonment of the gold exchange standard was now complete. With the bulk of the nation's gold stock in the possession of government, and its monopoly over our money supply established, it didn't take long for the government to exploit its position. The very day after the passage of this legislation, January 31, 1934, President Roosevelt reduced the gold content of the dollar by 40.94 per cent. The new price of gold was established at $35.00 per ounce in place of the old price of $20.67 per ounce.

Overnight the face value of the gold held by the Treasury and Federal Reserve Banks increased by almost three billion dollars. This devaluation directly repudiated forty per cent of the dollar claims to gold held by foreigners. The government wasted no time in getting started its engine of inflation. The American people were about to learn that only the discretion of the government money monopolists remained to limit the inflation of our money supply. It is a matter of historical record that not much discretion ever existed. The money supply has increased more than seventeen-fold since our abandonment of the gold exchange standard. The magnitude of this monetary expansion has reduced the purchasing power of today's paper dollar to about one quarter of its value in 1933.

During this era of continued inflation the government was severing any remaining legal ties to gold. The final tie was cut on August 15, 1971, when the "gold window" was closed to foreigners. After that date, not even foreign central banks could convert their dollar holdings to gold. The American dollar was nothing but irredeemable fiat money.

Still a Money Monopoly

The legalization of gold ownership today does not restore gold as a medium of exchange. As a matter of fact, the willingness of the state to once again permit gold ownership is precisely because the state no longer views gold as a threat to its money monopoly.

Gold can now be owned as a nonmonetary commodity. Any effort, however, by private citizens to re-introduce gold money as a medium of exchange will be promptly challenged by the government as illegal competition against its monopoly of paper money. Gold ownership was not legalized in order to restore a sound money, but instead, because government no longer considers gold important.

Overconfidence, however, even by a monopolist, can lead to a miscalculation. So, any relaxation of power by the State, any restoration of freedom to the citizenry, should be acclaimed with joy and fully exploited.

The restoration of the legal right to own gold is the action of an overconfident money monopolist. While the use of gold as a medium of exchange is still prohibited, the fact that we may own gold provides a means to protect our wealth from the ravages of inflation.

A Measure of Stability

If the State continues on its, inflationary path, cash holdings in paper money will be reduced, or even eliminated in some cases. Holding gold will be more advantageous. The expansion of the quantity of the government's paper money, which erodes its purchasing power, cannot touch gold. On the contrary, the price of gold may be expected to rise in direct reflection of the declining purchasing power of the paper dollar.

This development will become more and more visible. The advantage of holding gold rather than paper money will become obvious to all. Conversion from gold to paper money, in order to complete an exchange, and then converting back to gold from paper will become commonplace. While the process introduces an additional complication in our exchanges, buyers and sellers in the market will readily discover that this additional "complication" is a small burden to pay in order to offset the inflationary impact of government money.

This trading practice is widespread in those countries throughout the world that permit private ownership of gold while still suffering from chronic inflation. With lengthy histories of paper inflation as their lesson, people in foreign lands hold gold, not paper, in their secret hiding places. Gold's immunity from government generated inflation has made it a prized possession in these inflationary times.

Our exchange economy does not have to follow such dismal examples. Though not intended as such, the first step toward a return to sound money has been taken. As individuals begin to register their preference for gold over paper in the market, the next major step by our government must be considered: permitting gold as a medium of exchange. [2]

Leave It to the Market

Past intrusion by government into monetary affairs has only led to monetary destruction. While the law can guard money from fraud, it cannot create money. Money evolves from the market and the need for a means to facilitate our exchanges.

If individuals are to have their full freedom to make exchanges, they must also be free to determine the media in which their exchanges shall be made. Throughout history, gold has been the commodity chosen by free men to accomplish this end.

The legalization of gold ownership will allow the market to demonstrate that gold is the preferred media for making trades. Once again it will be seen that sound money can only originate within the market.

The final restoration of a sound money will require a major shift in political thinking. The futility of continued inflation must first be recognized. As the failure of "political money" becomes increasingly obvious to voters, government hopefully will abandon its monopoly power over the money system. In response to the public clamor for a sound money, gold will finally prevail.

The soundness of gold in contrast to the deterioration of paper money will be clear to all who care to see it. All that is required by government hereafter is the removal of legal barriers to free use of gold in trade. The competitive forces of the market will shortly re-establish it as the "market's money."

So, from the now restored right to own gold, we may hope eventually to reassert our right to use it as money, The welfare of all of us is dependent on such a result.

The survival of a free market is dependent on the preservation of a sound money. If sound money is to be restored and our freedom preserved, government must surrender its monopoly over money and allow gold to once again serve buyers and sellers in the market as our medium of exchange.

Gold is legal, but it is not yet money.

Economic Sophisms

Ever since the advent of representative government placed the ultimate power to direct the administration of public affairs in the hands of the people, the primary instrument by which the few have managed to plunder the many has been the sophistry that persuades the victims that they are being robbed for their own benefit. The public has been despoiled of a great part of its wealth and has been induced to give up more and more of its freedom of choice because it is unable to detect the error in the delusive sophisms by which protectionist demagogues, national socialists and proponents of government planning exploit its gullibility and its ignorance of economics.

About the Author

Arthur Goddard, from his preface to the English-language edition of Economic Sophisms by Frederic Bastiat.

At the time of the original publication, Mr. Anderson was Executive Secretary and Director of Seminars at the Foundation for Economic Education.

[1] B. M. Anderson, *Economics and the Public Welfare (Princeton, N. J.: D. Van Nostrand Company, Inc., 1959), pp. 348-49.*

[2] *See Hans F. Sennholz, Inflation, or Gold Standard?, "Return to the Gold Standard" (Lansing, Mich.: Bramble Minibooks, 1973).*

Reprinted with permission from The Freeman, a publication of The Foundation for Economic Education, Inc., January, 1975, Vol. 25, No. 1.

Letter from the Paper Planet

Ernest G. Ross

Dear Sir:

This is my first letter to you since arriving "incognito" several weeks ago here on The Paper Planet. When you suggested that traveling to this planet for the summer would be good experience for a student working toward his economics degree, I had no idea why you felt that way. I should have guessed. Given all the "experiments" with fiat monetary systems in which the nations of Earth have chosen to engage, "The Paper Planet" is indeed a good nickname for the place.

It would be an understatement for me to say I'm astonished. The extent of the mental contortions in which most of Earth's economists are willing to engage in order to justify paper money schemes strikes me as incredible. The extent of the deceptions and coercion in which the politicians are willing to indulge strikes me as downright barbaric! But, as one of our own great economists once stated, "The economists provide the seeds of monetary policies; the politicians merely sow." In that case, I suppose many of Earth's economists are equally guilty of barbarism.

But enough of my moralizing. Here is a summary of what I have observed. (Please understand, Professor - these observations are taken largely from my notes as I made them. I have not had time to formally organize my writing yet. Nevertheless, the pattern should be clear.)

As you know, all of the truly civilized planets have long ago adopted "hard money" standards - standards based generally on precious metals, usually gold, due to its store of value qualities of rarity, divisibility, relatively steady demand, and durability. Gold exists in normal amounts on Earth and would therefore be the logical choice for a monetary standard here.

However, despite actual experiences with the virtues of gold, almost all nations have abandoned this metal in favor of fiat paper currencies. The first purpose I set myself was to find out why.

The most common argument against a gold standard seems to be that it is "too limiting" to a nation's economy. Inasmuch as all planets' histories show that hard money standards are growth-promoting, I could not understand this claim at first.

Limiting Aspects of Gold

The key to comprehension of this amazing contention is to define what the Earthlings mean by "too limiting." Apparently it has two major meanings - economic and political. Often, on The Paper Planet, they are inextricably intertwined.

First, the economics.

A fiat standard of money can give the impression that it is possible to "force feed" an economy in order to achieve continuously high levels of stable growth. This force feeding is done by printing money in vast quantities and often involves subsidized interest rates. The idea is to give people more incentive to spend money and less incentive to save. And, indeed, this process does result in abnormal growth - for short periods of time.

But a couple of severe problems soon occur. More money in circulation (because the printing of money inevitably continues to exceed the rate of production of goods and services) results in a depreciation of purchasing power. This, in tandem with disincentives to save, erodes the capital base of a nation. Less capital - less quality capital, I should say - means less business investment, which means less growth and employment. This eventually leads to an economic contraction called a "recession."

Strangely, one of the early aims of flat systems was to prevent recessions! How this was to be accomplished is very vague - never adequately explained in all of Earth's economic literature. Personally, I believe that because such force feeding policies are in total violation of several economic laws, it is not at all surprising no one has been able to clearly explain the policies. At first, I thought that perhaps Earth-men were inordinately prone to wishful thinking. But that is not the case. What they are prone to is politics.

That brings us to the second interpretation of the phrase, "too limiting."

One of the hallmarks of our galaxy's civilized worlds is their universal restriction on money-tampering. I confess that until I visited The Paper Planet, I had a very incomplete understanding of the reason for this restriction. I want you to know, Professor, that I have thoroughly corrected that gap in my knowledge.

A hard money system keeps a check on politicians; it is their excesses that a gold standard limits. I have found that when a politician on Earth complains that hard money is "too limiting," it is simply his way of saying that he has reasons to embezzle the populace's wealth. Perhaps, Sir, that sounds a bit harsh; but in fact, that's what it all boils down to.

My supporting evidence:

Paper money systems always lead to inflation - and politicians always manage to construct tax systems to take advantage of this fact. As people demand higher wages to offset the erosion of their purchasing power, they are "pushed into higher tax brackets," meaning, they are taxed at increasingly steeper rates. The more taxes the politicians have at their disposal, the easier it becomes for them to "buy" the favors of special interest groups. Politicians are quite careful to buy these favors quietly (at least in the early stages of a fiat system - later on they can become embarrassingly brazen about it)--that is, they do not admit what they are doing. Instead, they use euphemisms as, "the public interest," "the common good," "the welfare of the people," "aiding the local economy," and "watching out for the folks back home."

Each special interest group (and almost everyone belongs to some such group inasmuch as it is natural for people to have special interests in certain things) finds it almost impossible to resist taking these favors from the politicians because the favors represent wealth far and above what any individual group believes it could otherwise acquire as quickly on its own. To justify acceptance, the recipients of this inflation-generated tax largess also have euphemisms, the more common of which are, "If we [or I don't accept it, someone else will," and, "We're just getting back a little of what we already paid in [in taxes]." As you can see, Sir, it is a very vicious cycle - and, I might point out, has historically led to the downfall of nation after nation on this planet.

Paper Money Policies

A few lines back, I mentioned the fact that paper money has (especially in the late Twentieth Century, the current hundred-year calendar period on Earth) been adopted partly on the idea that its judicious (!) use could prevent recessions. In light of The Paper Planet's brief recent historical experiences with hard money, this idea needs special attention. Flying in the face of evidence, modem politicians on Earth seem convinced that under a gold standard the "ups and downs" of an economy are much more severe than under a fiat standard. All I can say to this, Sir, is that whatever standard of judgment is at play is, to twist the meaning of an Earth colloquialism, "out of this world" - because it certainly hasn't come out of our hard money worlds!*

The facts: Under periods of hard money standards on The Paper Planet (a good example is the late Nineteenth Century in the geographical area called "The United States of America"), inflation-deflation had been up and down about two per cent (averaging out to zero, of course), while in the late Twentieth Century - paper money times - inflation has steadily increased from lows of two per cent in the immediate post- World War II period to highs of nearly 15 per cent in the late 1970s!

While some argument might be made that growth rates have been a little higher under the paper money system than under the gold standard (four or five per cent during "boom" times for the former, three or four per cent for the latter), the picture is quite distorted. Fiat currencies so disrupt the accounting procedures of the economy that the argument is specious at best - and does not take into account the higher, productivity - advancing technologies which leapt into existence in the 1970s; the subtle, but vast erosion of incentives to save - which, as mentioned earlier, plays havoc with a nation's future productivity; the enormous burdens of taxes which the inflation created, resulting in virtually no rise in the standard of living for nearly a dozen years.

As a student of economics, Professor, I admit I'm compelled to ask, "If fiat currencies really produce higher economic growth - as their advocates maintain - then why have living standards stagnated during the period of most explosive money growth?" Keep in mind, Sir, that these facts pertain to the nation which is thought to be the best off economically of all the major nations of The Paper Planet.

Already I miss my home-world. I cannot help but wistfully reminisce on the differences in everyday life at home and here on Earth.

At first, I was going to leave these reminiscences out of my letter. However, upon serious reflection, I believe they have instructive value - at least, they did for me; I'm sure you're already aware of these differences, Sir, or you never would have suggested this visit to Earth. So, bear with your Humble Student.

On the home-world, under our gold standard, businessmen have an enormous advantage over those here on The Paper Planet. The gold standard creates a climate of great stability and confidence in the future. Here, the erosion of money's value (as well as the periodic bouts of high interest rates when they are politically allowed to reflect inflation) creates an atmosphere of fear-fear of economic crashes and recessions, of renewed periods of stagnation, and of reduced purchasing power. These factors lead to other fears, especially fear of protectionism (and thus contracted trade and international ill will), which has often - I shudder to think of how often - led to war as the more tyrannical nations began to prey on the perceived corruption and weakening of the fabric of their wealthier neighbors. Often the attacks against their neighbors were used to distract attention from the tyrannies' own terrible economic problems.

On the home-world, entrepreneurship is a constant, normal, exciting part of our lives. With the stability of a hard money system (which, of course, helps keep taxes down) it is possible for most people, with a very few years of work, to raise enough capital to start their own businesses. This has resulted in virtually no forced (i.e., government-caused) unemployment.

It is hard to imagine a system under which individuals do not have the option of easily switching careers through entrepreneurship choice; it is almost impossible to imagine a system under which the people have come to expect government to take care of them when they are out of work, or forcefully "protect" their jobs by preventing businesses from failing (by law, no less!); it is downright distasteful, Sir, to see people who have become so dependent on government expropriation of their neighbors' wealth! Yet, that is exactly the kind of systems that dominate The Paper Planet. It is the kind of horrid dehumanization which happens from institutionalization of fiat currencies.

Related to the previous paragraph, on the home-world, we have no concept of "social security" - a system almost universally accepted on Earth as a way of guaranteeing that no one will be without means of support in his or her old age.

Reasons for Social Security

There are several reasons why this so-called "security system" has evolved as a direct result of paper currencies:

(1) With the loss of the entrepreneurship choice, it is impossible for most of the Planet's people to effectively generate large enough quantities of capital wealth to provide for their later years.

(2) The high tax rates generated by a fiat standard discourage savings even by a life-long wage earner; thus the non-entrepreneur, the person who doesn't like being an entrepreneur, is stripped of his means of self-provision. (This varies from nation to nation on The Paper Planet. In the United States, more than any other major nation, it would still be possible -though barely - for average wage earners to provide for their personal retirements, if they were allowed to keep the money which is now taxed for Social Security and instead put it into private retirement plans of their choice. There is a move in that direction now, but I fear that unless the paper money system is abandoned, the trend will grind to a halt.)

(3) The fiat system has so undercut the self-confidence of the people that it has largely instilled in them an actual (I believe inhuman) desire to be taken care of by government. That is a sad, sad state of affairs to witness, Sir. The horrible thing is, the more the government caters to this dependency, the worse it gets. In a perversion that perhaps best illustrates how serious the situation has become, most people now think of Social Security as a right!

On the home-world, even simple, everyday things are easier to accomplish than on The Paper Planet. A good example would be the way my wife is able to deal with our family's financial needs.

Because prices are so stable (of course, they actually fall a bit each year), she is able to logically, confidently plan our home's future. As most families do on the home-world, we can reasonably project when we'll be able to buy new furniture, purchase a new family vehicle or new entertainment/communications equipment, acquire a finer home, and so forth.

More importantly to us, we know that we'll be able to finance our two children's education (presuming they want our help - - little Suzy and Johnny are showing signs of dedicated independence!). Sir, did you know that on Earth, most graduate students cannot even consider starting families for years? They are simply too poor to do so. I cannot imagine suffering the poverty they endure; I don't know what I would have done without the option of free-lancing work for home-world financial institutions while going to college; it's wonderful to be able to earn enough money to raise a family and pay for my education out of such part-time work - truly an indication of how a hard money system raises living standards!

Faith in the Future

While the spirit of the future, underscored by the constant introduction of thousands and thousands of innovations, permeates the world view of the average citizen of the home-world and our sister planets, here on The Paper Planet, that spirit is a frustrated, deformed thing, where it exists at all. At home, under the venture-capital-encouraging hard money system, innovations are not abnormal-they are virtually taken for granted! As you know, we all expect that each year we will personally have newer, better products from which to choose. It is a condition which my father and grandfather enjoyed - and their fathers and grandfathers before them for many generations. It is a condition which we regard as one of the great joys of our hard money system. To witness the bountiful fruit of human ingenuity flooding our markets each year - what could be more inspiring to an individual?

I suppose, Sir, that my letter from The Paper Planet would be somewhat incomplete if I did not mention how Earth could, in my view, rid itself of this "paper pestilence."

Having spent several weeks with Earthlings, and despite their stubbornly uncivilized monetary ways, I have grown rather fond of them. While - as on all worlds - there are evil people scattered about, most Earth people are basically decent, and if given half a chance in the ordinary courses of their lives, show a promising respect for the rights of others. I believe this "gut level" respect could be solidified in a major way if even one nation - especially an influential, large nation - were to return to the discipline of gold. Gold cements the right of property, which in many ways underlies all other rights - hence, the idea that a gold standard would assist in institutionalizing a respect for rights. It would make for a much better planet Earth.

The United States Could Lead

As far as I can tell, the most likely candidate for a return to a hard money system is the United States of America. This nation is still the freest of all the large nations, and has recently undertaken greater discipline of its fiat currency - a currency which, it is important to note, is virtually the "base" or "reserve" currency of all other major, non-totalitarian trading nations.

However, because of the insidious nature of the politics constantly engendered under a fiat money standard, I fear this new discipline cannot last. At least, it will not unless it is underpinned by something more than the resolve of politicians - as attracted as they are to a fiat standard's "constituency-buying," special-interest-catering qualities. So, clearly, that underpinning ought to be a hard currency - -probably both gold and silver.

Because the United States is also the most advanced nation technologically, and is considered the leading nation of the planet, a return to a gold standard would be the fastest avenue for helping Earth to gain many of the same benefits which we on the home-world now take for granted. The U.S. lead in technology would allow industry to most rapidly expand under the stability a gold standard would provide; U.S. "leader" status would, by example, and by the greatly increased value of its already respected (though fatally flawed) fiat currency, spread the benefits of a new, hard currency system to the rest of the world. In a sense, the American dollar is the circulatory system of world trade. Putting gold into the system would be like increasing the oxygen-carrying capacity of blood-infusing world trade with new energy and vitality.

Steps Back to Gold

While there are undeniably many ways in which U.S. leaders could accomplish this conversion from a "soft" to a "hard" standard of money, the best way would have to involve these three factors:

(1) Allowing free private ownership of gold (already in effect in America).

(2) Tying the dollar to a specific weight of gold or silver - and allowing people to convert back and forth.

Convertibility is absolutely necessary if the citizens are to have a, "veto" over political money-tampering. When citizens can exchange dollars for specific weights of gold or silver, the burden is on the government to refrain from inflating - for if it does reflate, citizens will drain the government's valuable gold reserves. Of course, when point number three is implemented, private coinage will provide the final check on politicians: taking the governance and responsibility for maintaining the integrity of money out of their hands entirely. This, of course, is our system on the home-world.

(3) Ultimately permitting private coinage of gold and making no laws barring the use of privately minted coins in trade or banking.

Well, Sir, that about wraps it up. I'll present a more detailed report to you in further letters and in person when I return to the home-world. Thank you for suggesting my visit to The Paper Planet. It is a visit which will undoubtedly remain as one of the most important experiences of my life. My only hope is that the residents of this lovely planet Earth learn as much about the nature of their fiat systems as I have. Until they do, I fear they will remain mired in an immature culture and may very well lose an immense amount of the progress they've already gained.

Sincerely,

Your Humble Student

*Although hard money has limited recent experience, it was quite extensively used in more ancient Earth - for example, as Why Gold? (Exposition Press, 1974) author, Leslie Snyder, wrote of the Byzantine Empire, "The bezant [unit of currency] was minted at a standard of 65 grains of fine gold for 800 years ... So determined were the empire's rulers to maintain the integrity of their money that they required all bankers and others through whose hands money passed to take an oath never to file, clip or debase coins in any manner. The penalty for any violation of this oath: the offender's hand was cut off." This, unfortunately, was the longest recorded use of an uncorrupted gold standard. Even in the ancient world, gold standards did not long remain inviolate from the tamperings of politicians.

About the Aurhor

At the time of the original publication, Mr. Ross was an Oregon commentator and writer especially concerned with new developments in human freedom.

Reprinted with permission from The Freeman, a publication of the Foundation for Economic Education, Inc., October 1983, Vol. 33, No. 10.

Precious Metals Investing Tips

Adam Starchild

Investment in precious metals always has been largely a reflection of an individual's perception of the direction of national and world events. While momentary speculators jumped in and out of markets hoping for a quick killing, the long-term prudent investor makes an effort to understand the fundamental factors that govern economic interaction. He or she becomes thoroughly versed in the history, current state, and prospects for their considered investment - whether stocks and bonds, real property, commodities futures or - precious metals.

History supports the fact that at various times investment in tangible commodities is the best protection against the future.

"Mine! All mine!"

Like King Midas of the fabled "golden touch," many investors prefer personal physical possession of their gold, allowing tangible control of their asset. Pride of ownership also moves investors to have their gold within reach so they can display it for friends, or just admire it in the comfort of their hopefully security alarm-equipped home.

If you find the idea of physical possession of gold appealing, you may want to buy the metal in the form of gold bars or privately minted coin-like commemorative medallions.

The standard unit of gold in international trading between banks and governments is the 400-troy ounce (12.5 kilogram) bar of a fineness of 995/1000, with an identifying serial number stamp, traditionally referred to as a London "good delivery bar".

One troy ounce is equal to 1.09714 regular ounce avoir du pois. The troy ounce is a special measurement of gold with ancient Anglo-Saxon origins equaling 31.1035 metric grams of gold. The purest gold of 999.9 fineness is used in the making of these smaller bars.

Gold bullion bars are available in at least 20 sizes and weights ranging from a tiny one-gram bar, known as a "wafer," and a pocket-sized kilobar (32.15 troy ounces), to the large 400 troy ounce London "good delivery bar" valued at $145,000 (at $362.50 an ounce). This wide size variety offers a spread in gold bar prices, providing opportunities for investors of small or large amounts of capital.

In addition to the advantages of having gold under one's own immediate control, there are several good reasons favoring investment in gold bullion; commissions paid on the buying and selling of bullion are minimal; re-sale of bullion bearing the marks of reputable refiners is relatively easy; and bullion prices are uniformly quoted throughout the world. Gold bullion also may be purchased from thousands of outlets at precious metals dealers, metals exchange companies, major banks and many brokerage firms.

Gold Coins - A Universal Treasure:

Gold coins have fascinated the world's investors for more than two thousand years, probably since soon after King Gyges of Lydia ordered the first ones minted in 670 BC.

There are two main types of gold coins: 1) rare or "numismatic" coins prized by collectors, the value of which is enhanced by their scarcity and is a matter of subjective judgment; 2) bullion or intrinsic coins, always government-issued, which are not scarce and sell at only nominal additional premiums over the actual value of their gold metallic content. It is this second class of gold coins which are the most practical for the investor, since they can be bought and sold easily in varying quantities at a price known worldwide.

Investors purchase gold coins because it is an easy way to satisfy the need for physical possession of their gold. The popularity of such coins, and privately minted coin-like medallions, can be attributed to the small size, convenient weights, security and ease of storage and transportation.

In addition to their intrinsic value, many ancient gold coins are both rare antiquities and miniature works of art, bought and sold within the worldwide numismatic collecting community at prices well above the value of their gold content. Rare coins are private and do not require the filing of IRS reports as do gold bullion transactions. Although numismatic gold and gold bullion both increase in value in times of inflation, rare gold coins also increase in value during non-inflationary periods of general prosperity. For example, from 1987 through 1989, the price of gold fell from over $500 an ounce to $350, at a time when a representative index of numismatic gold more than doubled in value.

There are also many collectable government-minted gold legal tender coins issued in limited quantities to commemorate events or persons of national historical importance. The typical gold bullion coin is legal tender within the issuing nation, and its gold content is government guaranteed. In many cases these coins bear a largely symbolic numerical face value and their true market value depends totally on the actual percentage of gold content.

Owners of gold bullion coins or privately issued medallions can easily keep track of their current value because most popular gold "pieces" or "rounds," as they are sometimes called, contain one "troy ounce" of pure gold, the price of which is reported daily in the financial section of most newspapers.

Bullion coins of less than a full troy ounce are minted in convenient fractional weights including one-half, one-quarter, and one-tenth ounces. Among the countries issuing gold bullion coins, now or in the past, are Australia, Austria, the Republic of South Africa, Canada, China, Great Britain, Hungary, Mexico and the United States.

The purchase price of bullion coins normally includes a 3 to 5 percent premium over the true value of the gold content, but this increase generally will be recovered at resale.

Bullion coins and privately minted gold medallions can be purchased at banks, precious metals dealers, brokerage firms and jewelers. The smaller gold bullion coins have become an increasingly popular type of investment jewelry, and it is not uncommon to see a person wearing one attached to a matching 24kt gold chain.

One of the best sources for gold coins and bullion is a broker/ dealer founded in 1982 by two of the former senior officers of

Deak-Perera, at the time the nation's oldest and largest precious metals and foreign exchange firm. Asset Strategies International, Inc., Suite 400A, 1700 Rockville Pike, Rockville MD 20852 are not "coin dealers," meaning that they don't take positions in the precious metals therefore creating a bias to sell certain items. Instead, through their domestic and international network of wholesalers they buy and sell at competitive prices. They can be called in the USA and in Canada on a toll free line (800) 831-0007 for current market quotes or general information.

Clients and friends of the firm receive their monthly newsletter, Information Line, free of charge. The publication will keep you up-to-date on the precious metals and foreign exchange markets.

They are well known in the financial newsletter industry and at one time or another have been recognized as a "recommended vendor" by many of the writers in the newsletter industry. The principals, Michael Checkan and Glen Kirsch have been in the precious metals/foreign exchange business for a combined total of 50 years.

Investment Without Immediate Possession:

If a prospective investor values convenience and ease of ownership transfer over actual physical possession of gold, there are available a wide variety of bank-issued gold certificates, accumulation plans, futures contracts and options, gold mining stocks, and mutual and other gold investment funds.

Issued by many banks, "gold certificates" obligate the bank to deliver a stated quantity and fineness of gold to the holder in accordance with the certificate's exact terms and conditions. Financial institutions issue these certificates in fractional denominations, offering the opportunity to invest in convenient dollar amounts.

Buying gold certificates is a simple process. There usually are no fabrication or delivery charges, and while your bullion is on deposit with the institution, insurance coverage is provided. Regular customer statements provide the approximate current value of your gold investment, and the issuing institution is obligated to deliver that amount of gold at any time you wish, or you can order them to sell the certificate.

Perth Mint Certificate Program

There is a little-known way to hold gold and other precious metals overseas, privately. It's called the Perth Mint Certificate Program (PMCP), and it is an excellent way to ensure your wealth securely, discreetly, flexibly and inexpensively.

When you buy precious metals in the PMCP, you get a certificate of ownership. The certificate represents a specific item the bullion or coins you purchased. The Perth Mint sets aside a certain amount of a specific material for use at your sole and personal discretion. The document simply shows "ounce for ounce" what you own that the Perth Mint is holding for you.

The PMCP is an extremely private way to own precious metals. The PMCP is not considered a foreign bank or financial account abroad. Therefore, precious metals stored at the PMCP (in a non-banking depository) are not reportable, even though the program allows you to transfer wealth from one part of the world to another. The PMCP is not considered a monetary instrument, since it is non-negotiable and does not provide a payment of a "sum certain" in dollars. In legal terms it is a "warehouse receipt". Your assets and any related documents are stored offshore (in Perth). You retain the ownership certificates, which are transferable but non-negotiable.

In case of an economic catastrophe, you simply use the documents to request delivery from Perth to any number of major financial centers, such as Zurich, London, or Singapore.

Some countries have restrictions on gold ownership, but you may remove your assets from the Perth Mint whenever you wish. When you receive the coins, you can cross country borders without duty (unlike bullion, which is not always duty free). There are no import or export duties on precious metals in Australia. Coins purchased in the PMCP enjoy worldwide recognition you can liquidate them in any major financial market (subject to import restrictions).

The program also allows you your choice of gold, silver, platinum and palladium. No other certificate program we've researched offers all four metals. And, you can sell all or part of your holdings and receive your proceeds in a variety of currencies: U.S. dollars, Australian dollars, Swiss francs, or other major foreign currencies. All precious metals transactions are completed based on the London p.m. fix.

The PMCP's products the highest quality and purity Australian semi-numismatic coins come in various sizes, ranging from 1/20 oz. to 1 kilo (gold, platinum, and silver are available in the 1 kilo size). The PMCP offers low premiums low storage charges and a $50 certificate charge (per transaction). The bigger the transaction the bigger the savings. Of all the available precious metal buy-and-store programs, the PMCP offers the most inexpensive way to buy precious metals, privately, in a convenient form. Now there is an easy way to hold part of your portfolio in precious metals, and get the benefits of global diversification.

For more information on the exclusive Perth Mint Certificate Program, contact:

> Asset Strategies International, Inc.
> 1700 Rockville Pike, Suite 400A
> Rockville MD 20852
>
> Telephone: (800) 831-0007
> Fax: (301) 881-1936

Michael Checkan and Glen Kirsch of Asset Strategies International are well known in the financial newsletter industry and at one time or another have been recognized as a "recommended vendor" by many of the writers in the newsletter industry. Among the many writers and publications recommending them are Mark Skousen, Richard Band, Adrian Day, International Living, and Taipan. Adrian Day, editor of Adrian Day's Investment Analyst says "I've frequently recommended Michael and Glen in the past; you can continue to have confidence in utilizing their services." The principals, Michael Checkan and Glen Kirsch, have been in the foreign exchange business for a combined total of 50 years. They helped the Perth Mint to design this certificate program, using their decades of experience with precious metals and other certificate programs.

Afterword
Perth Mint Certificate Program Highlights

- *Low certificate fees - U.S.$50.00 per certificate*

- *Low storage fees for allocated precious metals - 1/2% per annum*

- *NO storage fees for unallocated precious metals - requires 1 week's notice for delivery*

- *Low program minimums - U.S.$25,000 to open, U.S.$5,000 or more to add*

- *No import or export duties on precious metals in Australia*

- *Extremely competitive pricing*

Reliable...

The Perth Mint is a division of Gold Corporation, wholly owned and operated by the Western Australia Government, so your metals are government guaranteed.

Discreet...

Private vaulting relationships overseas require no U.S. government reporting, unlike foreign bank accounts.

Storage agreements between the Perth Mint and its clients are coded specifically to the client through the use of a password, client number, and Perth Mint Certificate number.

Secure...

Since 1899, the Perth Mint has provided safe storage of precious metals.

Storage is primarily available in Perth, Western Australia, one of the most politically and economically stable of the continents.

Precious metals are insured (at Perth Mint's expense) by Lloyd's of London.

Flexible...

No pre-determined document sizes!

Storage is available for all precious metals (gold, silver, platinum and palladium).

Storage can be on an allocated or an unallocated basis.

Delivery is offered in a variety of locations world-wide.

PMCP Certificates are non-negotiable, but they are transferable.

Storage options can be changed to meet the investor's changing needs.

Tax Strategies For Precious Metals Investors

You may have purchased bullion coin investments in the 1970s and 1980s at prices substantially higher than today's levels. For instance, gold is now trading in the $400 per ounce range, less than half of its historic high of more than $800 per ounce. Silver is also trading much lower than its previous peaks. These low prices in tangible assets may not last for long.

Because stock "wash sale" rules do not apply Asset Strategies International, Inc. has developed a program that enables you to take advantage of today's low prices to reduce your tax burden by taking losses on your coin investments to offset current ordinary income, or to shelter gains that you have realized on your other investments. Investors owning bullion coins that have declined in value can sell those coins to Asset Strategies, thereby creating a deductible loss, and will have the option, but not the obligation, to buy the same coins back from Asset Strategies, or can buy other, materially different coins or metals from Asset Strategies.

Provided that the transaction meets the criteria set forth in the laws and regulations, any loss resulting from your sale or exchange can be deducted up to $3,000 of ordinary income, or can be deducted against capital gains on other investments, with the ability to carry unused losses forward to future years. This deduction will be available even if you exercise your option to repurchase the coins from Asset Strategies. Contact Asset Strategies International, Inc., Suite 400A, 1700 Rockville Pike, Rockville MD 20852.

About the Author

Adam Starchild is the author of over a dozen books, and hundreds of magazine articles, primarily on business and finance. His articles have a appeared in a wide range of publications around the world — including Business Credit, Euromoney, Finance, The Financial Planner, International Living, Offshore Financial Review, Reason, Tax Planning International, Trusts & Estates, and many more. His personal website is on the Internet at http://www.adamstarchild.com/